Quiltmaking
Essentials 1

Quiltmaking
Essentials 1

Cutting and Piecing Skills

Donna Lynn Thomas

Martingale®
Create with Confidence

Dedication

To the memory of my mother, who passed on her love of sewing to me. Although she sewed clothing and I sew quilts, the love was truly shared. I hope some day when they are old enough, I can pass the same love on to my granddaughters, Charlotte and Alexandra.

Quiltmaking Essentials 1: Cutting and Piecing Skills
© 2014 by Donna Lynn Thomas

Martingale®
19021 120th Ave. NE, Ste. 102
Bothell, WA 98011-9511 USA
ShopMartingale.com

Printed in China

19 18 17 16 15 14   8 7 6 5 4 3 2 1

Library of Congress Cataloging-in-Publication Data is available upon request.

ISBN: 978-1-60468-440-7

Mission Statement

Dedicated to providing quality products and service to inspire creativity.

Credits

PRESIDENT AND CEO: Tom Wierzbicki

EDITOR IN CHIEF: Mary V. Green

DESIGN DIRECTOR: Paula Schlosser

MANAGING EDITOR: Karen Costello Soltys

ACQUISITIONS EDITOR: Karen M. Burns

TECHNICAL EDITOR: Laurie Baker

COPY EDITOR: Marcy Heffernan

PRODUCTION MANAGER: Regina Girard

COVER AND INTERIOR DESIGNER: Connor Chin

PHOTOGRAPHER: Brent Kane

ILLUSTRATOR: Anne Moscicki

Acknowledgments

Deep appreciation and thanks to Robin Fleming and Prym Consumer USA for providing much of the rotary equipment for photography.

A big thank-you to Georgia Gale of Needle and I (Everett, Washington) for providing my favorite Bernina for photography as well. Becky Keck, northwest regional manager for Bernina of America, took time from her busy schedule to make arrangements for the sewing machine. Thank you, Becky!

Contents

Introduction

This book is a reference manual about rotary cutting and machine-sewn patchwork, not appliqué, paper piecing, hand piecing, or foundation piecing. This volume (volume 1) covers basic rotary cutting, sewing, pressing, and block assembly. Volume 2 covers quilt-top assembly, sashes, borders, backings, and bindings.

Since we're talking about basics, let's begin at the beginning. What is a quilt? Well, it's not a blanket! A blanket is a single-layer, woven bed covering. While quilts are also traditionally thought of as bed covers, they're used extensively in home decor, decorating tables and walls, and are also seen more and more in museums as works of art.

Different from a blanket, a quilt is composed of two or three layers consisting most often of a patterned top, a batting (sometimes called a filling), and a backing (sometimes called a lining). The three layers are stitched together with decorative quilting stitches. This stitching is what gives a quilt its name, while the three layers give it the warmth. A two-layer summer quilt omits the middle layer and is often found in warmer climates.

Quilt tops can be constructed in a number of ways. A whole-cloth quilt is just what its name implies—one large piece of fabric, either plain or printed, that serves as the top. The decorative quilting provides the design.

Patchwork tops come in two forms: pieced or appliquéd. Appliqué is the process of cutting pieces of fabric and applying them to a larger whole to create a design. *Broderie perse* is one form of appliqué in which motifs are cut from printed fabrics and then applied to a whole cloth to form a design. Most

often today, though, pieces are appliquéd to smaller blocks, both plain and pieced, that are then sewn together to make the quilt top.

Appliquéd block

Piecing consists of sewing smaller pieces of fabric together side by side to form a greater whole. Most often, pieces are sewn into blocks of specific patterns that are then joined to make the quilt top. Sometimes pieces are sewn together into one overall design.

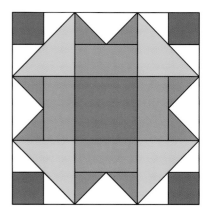

Pieces sewn together to form a block

Pieces sewn together to form an overall design

You'll find many references to precision in this book. Precision is *not* about pleasing the quilt police. It has everything to do with mastering skills so you can enjoy the process of making your beautiful quilts without frustration, mistakes, ripping, easing, and fudging to make things work. Remember, even Van Gogh had to learn how to hold a brush and mix paints before he could create his masterpieces. If you master precision skills so they become second nature, frustration-free sewing will be like breathing—you won't even think about it.

To help you learn the finer points of quiltmaking, you'll find four different types of tip boxes sprinkled throughout this book:

? **Did You Know?** tips explain words, concepts, or background information in a bit more depth.

🎗 **Blue-Ribbon Skills** tips offer suggestions for fine-tuning a particular skill.

! **Problem Solving** tips warn you of or help you out of a potential "oops" and suggest how to fix or prevent a problem.

**The Numbers Box** tip, everyone's favorite, will help you with—yikes!—math or numbers.

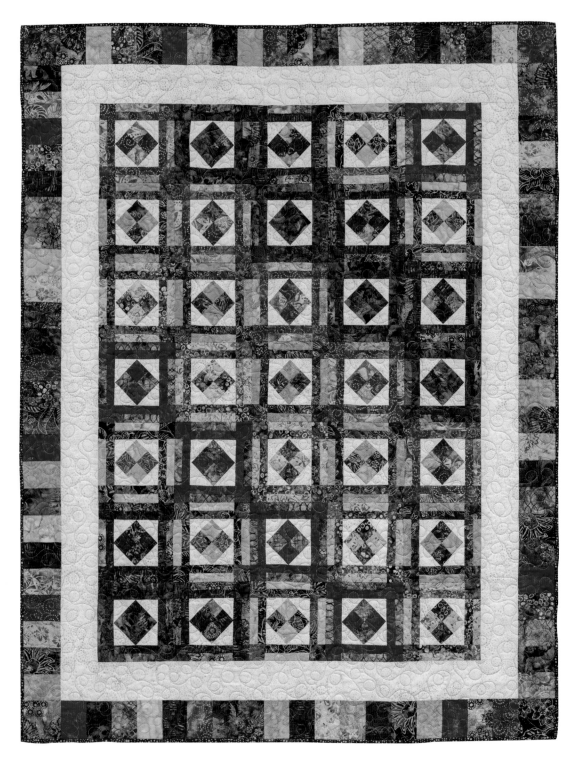

"Artifacts," pieced and quilted by Kim Pope, from *On-Point Patchwork*

Basic Concepts

Before you can dive in and start working on your first quilt, there are a few things worth reviewing. In this section, I'll cover the basic parts of a quilt, information on fabric, grain lines, fabric preparation, and threads. Entire books have been written on these subjects, so I'll try to keep it simple. I know you're anxious, but don't skip this section!

Parts of a Quilt

Other than an overall design (see page 7), most pieced quilt tops consist of blocks that are sewn together to make the top. Many tops, but not all, have sashing strips between the blocks and borders around the joined blocks, which are all identified in the illustration below. Sashing strips, borders, and

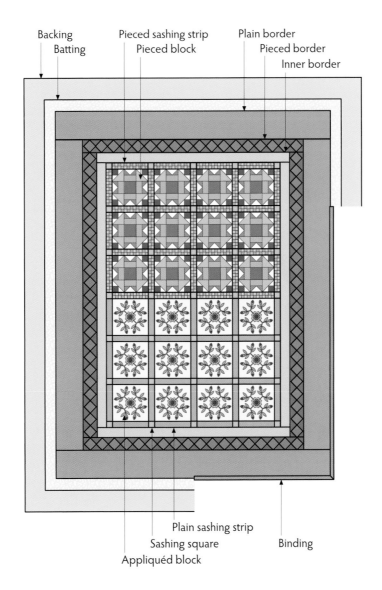

Backing
Batting
Pieced sashing strip
Pieced block
Plain border
Pieced border
Inner border

Plain sashing strip
Sashing square
Binding
Appliquéd block

backings can be plain or pieced. The binding is what encloses and finishes the outer edges of the quilt. In some cases, it too can be pieced for design considerations.

Fabric

Generally speaking, quilts are made from high-quality cotton fabric, although we're starting to see more and more quilts that make use of silk, linen, lamé, and other specialty fabrics for embellishment or creative effect. As this is a book about basics, we'll deal strictly with the use of cotton.

Essentially, there are two grades of quilting cotton: craft quality and quilt-shop quality. Both have their place. Craft quality isn't as expensive as quilt-shop quality, and for good reason. It's geared more toward short-term, nondurable craft items. For a quilt that's meant to last for many years, be sure to purchase quilt-shop-quality fabric. The dyes are less likely to run and are longer lasting, and the greige goods (base fabric) used in the manufacturing process are of much higher quality. With all the work that goes into making a quilt, it's worth the extra price for good-quality material to ensure it will last.

Most quilter's cottons are manufactured to be about 44" to 45" wide from selvage to selvage. As a general rule, you don't want to assume that you have any more than 40" to 42" of usable width after selvages are removed, especially if you prewash your fabrics.

> ### ? Did You Know?
>
> **The word selvage,** also spelled *selvedge*, is derived from the old weaving phrase "self edge."

Fabric Preparation

To prewash or not—that's always the subject of much heated discussion. I understand the arguments in both camps, but in the end I rarely prewash my fabric for a number of reasons.

Contrary to popular belief, prewashing will *not* fix a bleeding fabric—only a dye fixative will do that. Washing will remove surface dye, but we now have dryer sheets that will catch that extra dye when the finished quilt is washed, so I feel no need to prewash for that particular reason.

If I suspect that a particular fabric will bleed, I test a swatch of it in a jar of hot water for about 20 minutes. If it turns out to be a bleeder, then I'll treat it in a dye-fixative bath. Because that one fabric has now been preshrunk, all the fabric going into the quilt with it needs to be preshrunk as well.

> ### ! Problem Solving
>
> To prevent loss of dyes in cotton fabrics, do not use laundry detergents for washing; only use soaps. With repeated use, detergents can actually break down the bond between cotton and the dye, resulting in fading and color loss. Use a quilt soap as directed on the container, or add ½ cup of plain sudsy ammonia to the washer tub after it has filled with water and before you add the fabric. If you have a front-load washer, add the ammonia or quilt soap to the liquid dispenser, diluting the soap with a cup of water to make it less pasty. *Do not* use both products together.

Likewise, if you're mixing different weights of cotton fabric in a quilt, it's imperative that you prewash in order to preshrink. Different weights of fabric will shrink at different rates when the quilt is eventually washed, which could be disastrous. It's best to preshrink mixed fabric types.

Grain Line

Even though modern fabrics are made on highly sophisticated machinery, the basic process is little different from early history. Long warp yarns are tightly secured on each end of the loom and weft yarns are then woven side to side through the warp yarns to create the fabric, which is later printed or dyed. Due to the weaving, fabric has different grain-line properties.

Weft:
44" to 45"

Warp

Selvage

Selvage

Bias

The long, tightly secured warp yarns form the selvage. The grain running parallel to the selvage is called the lengthwise grain. It has little to no give when you pull on it. The less tightly secured weft yarns are called the crosswise grain. There is a bit

of stretch to this grain. Both lengthwise and cross-wise grains are generally referred to as the straight of grain.

The tricky grain line is the bias that runs at a 45° angle to the straight of grain. It has a considerable amount of stretch and can become distorted when overhandled. Take care when handling the bias edges of patchwork pieces.

The most important rule about grain line is that, as much as possible, all pieces parallel to the edges of the block should be cut on the straight grain so that the completed block won't easily stretch out of shape. As with any rule, sometimes you'll need to make exceptions.

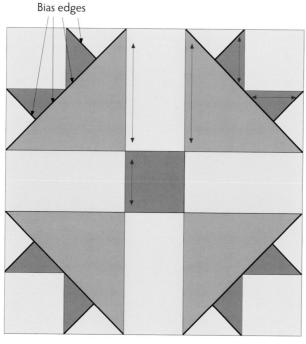

Bias edges

Red arrows indicate straight of grain.
Edges at 45° angle to straight of grain are bias.

Threads

The best thread for machine piecing is high-quality cotton thread. You'll find beautiful synthetic threads used in all manner of quilting and embellishment on the surface of the quilt. Why not use these for piecing as well? Part of the reason for the desirability of cotton thread for piecing is that it's weaker than polyester threads. This might not make sense until you consider that the seams joining all the little pieces in a quilt can come under a lot of stress. It's far better for the thread to break under high stress than for the fabric to tear. A seam can be sewn again but torn fabric isn't so easy to fix. This doesn't mean you'll want to use weak thread that breaks easily, causing seams to come apart willy-nilly. You need thread that will hold the seam together well, but that will also give under extreme stress before the fabric tears.

Just as with fabric, there are differences in the quality of the cotton that makes up different threads. Look for long-staple Egyptian cotton. It's more expensive than short-staple cotton, but it's worth it for its durability. Short-staple cotton is generally fairly inexpensive but it pulls apart easily, creating more lint in your machine.

> ## ? Did You Know?
>
> **Staple** indicates the actual cotton fiber in the cotton boll. Short staple means the fibers are short and when twisted together, they can separate easily. Long-staple fibers, when twisted, are less inclined to pull apart. The longer the staple, the stronger the thread.

Thread comes in different weights ranging from 10 to 100. The higher the number, the finer or thinner the thread, with 10 being very heavy and 100 the finest. Silk thread is generally 100 weight. Decorative embroidery, embellishment, and quilting threads tend toward the 10 to 40 weight range. The best weights for piecing are 50 and 60 weight.

Thread also comes in different plies. A ply indicates the number of cotton yarns that are twisted together to make the thread. For piecing, look for 2 or 3 ply. Thread that has the code 50/2 printed on the spool means that it's a 50-weight, 2-ply thread—perfect for piecing. Some 3-ply threads can actually be finer than a 2 ply if the initial yarns are finer. A 60-weight 3-ply thread can be finer than a 50-weight 2-ply thread. Look carefully at what you're buying.

The twist of the thread matters too, although most manufacturers don't put that information on the spools. The more twists per meter, the more durable and smooth the thread. You'll recognize a loosely twisted thread, as it tends to be coarser and will unravel easily in your hand. To make more twists requires more yarn content, so high-twist threads are therefore more costly.

Unlike in garment construction, quilters don't match thread color to fabric color, because we're usually sewing so many different-colored fabrics together. Instead, choose neutral-colored threads in grays, tans, blacks, or creams that work well with what you're sewing. For instance, if the fabrics are more tan-based than gray, use tan thread instead of a gray thread. If you're using a lot of white-based prints, use white or cream thread. Never use thread that's darker than the darkest print or lighter than the lightest print. If your machine stitches are appropriately sized with good tension, there shouldn't be any show-through of the thread on the seams.

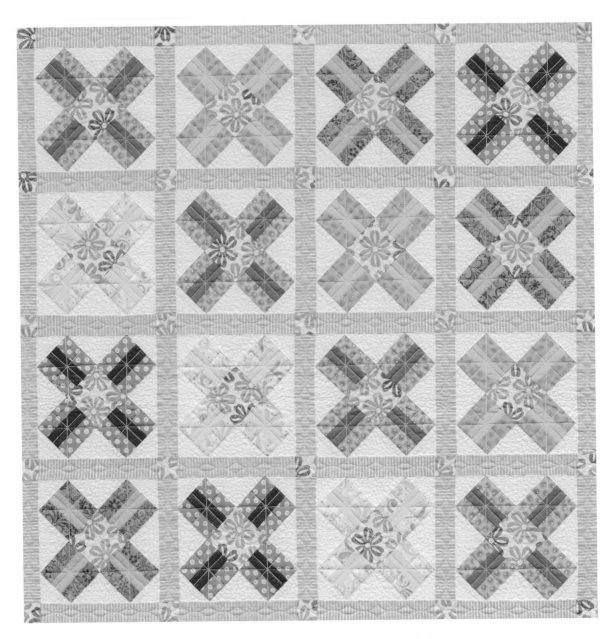

"Boxes and Bows," pieced by Donna Lynn Thomas and quilted by Denise Mariano, from *On-Point Patchwork*

Rotary Cutting

Cutting the pieces for a patchwork quilt used to require finished-size templates (pattern pieces transferred to a more durable substance such as cardboard or plastic) for each shape in the quilt block. A quilter would place the templates on the wrong side of fabrics and trace around them with a pencil. Using scissors, she'd cut the pieces ¼" from the marked line to create a seam allowance. The pencil marks became the sewing lines. Quilters would sew the pieces together by lining up the pencil lines and stitching by hand or machine.

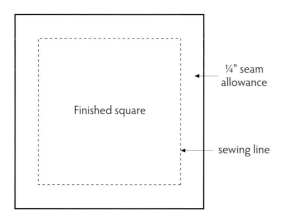

¼" seam allowance

Finished square

sewing line

With the advent of the rotary cutter, quilters have mostly abandoned templates. There are still some situations where templates are the best choice for marking what needs to be cut, but today you can find many amazing ⅛"-thick hard acrylic templates that make it possible to use a rotary cutter to cut the pieces instead of tracing and cutting with scissors.

When rotary cutting, you cut patchwork pieces that are equal to the finished size of the unit, plus an extra amount to account for the ¼" seam allowances used to sew the pieces together. So, when planning a pieced block, you need to know the finished sizes of your pieces as well as what to add for seam allowances in different situations. When working with commercial patterns, the calculations are done for you—just follow the cutting instructions. If you're working on your own design, the information you need to know is presented here.

Amazing precision and speed are possible with rotary cutting, which accounts for its popularity over many decades. Even so, basic skills must be mastered in order to achieve both speed and accuracy.

Equipment

The many varieties of rotary cutters, mats, and rulers available to today's quilters can be overwhelming. There are some basic features you need to be aware of, but beyond that, it's all gravy and icing (not a pretty mix, but you get the idea!).

Rotary Cutters

A rotary cutter is a cutting instrument with a round blade attached to a handle. It looks very much like a pizza cutter and works in the same fashion, only to cut fabric. Rotary cutters come in many sizes, shapes, and colors as well as different ergonomic designs.

Olfa introduced the first rotary cutter in 1979 for use in the garment industry. Quilters adopted it immediately and thus revolutionized quiltmaking by using it to create all kinds of innovative construction techniques. Today's cutters can be fitted with blades that cut different shapes such as scallops or pinked edges, along with the standard straight cut.

A good cutter should have a protective safety shield that's manually engaged and released. Some cutters have locks that prevent the blade from being engaged without the flip of a switch. If you have

Rotary cutters are available in many sizes and shapes.

small children or cats, I strongly recommend a cutter with all the safety bells and whistles even though you diligently keep the cutter out of reach. Don't purchase a cutter with a blade that you expose to cut simply by pushing down on it. It's too easy for little hands or paws to smack or grip a cutter, exposing the blade in the process. Such a cutter dropped on a hand or bare foot will protract the blade and cut upon impact. Rotary cuts can be dangerous. Please keep the safety engaged at all times when not actually cutting.

Periodically, you'll need to replace the rotary blade due to a nick or the dullness that comes with lots of use. Don't wait too long to replace a blade. A dull blade will slowly ruin your cutting mat, make it harder to cut through multiple layers, and require more pressure by the quilter to make the cuts, which can leave you all tuckered out before the job is halfway done! You'll be surprised at just how dull your blade was once you're using a fresh, new blade again.

Between replacements, keep your blade sharp and lasting longer by periodically cleaning the lint from between the blade and the safety shield using a soft cotton cloth. Before reassembling the cutter, put a drop of sewing-machine oil between the blade and the shield.

Problem Solving

When dismantling the cutter and blade, take each part off and lay it out in order of disassembly on a table. Then when you're ready to put it back together, pick up the parts and reassemble in reverse order. Follow this guideline, and you won't put the parts back in the wrong order.

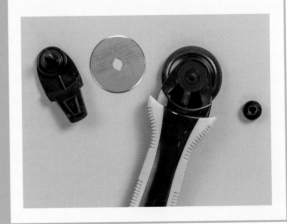

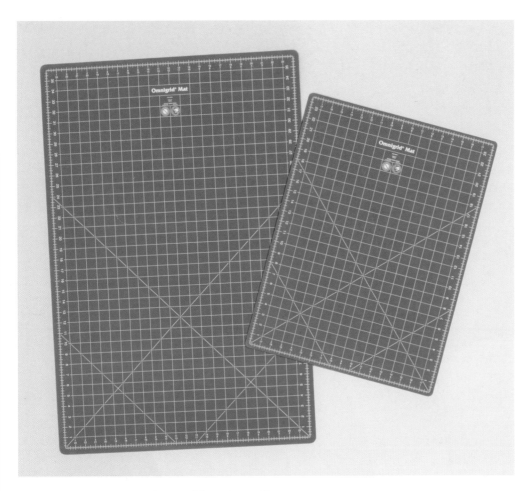

Rotary-cutting mats are designed for using with rotary cutters.

Rotary-Cutting Mats

A rotary-cutting mat is a self-healing mat designed for use with rotary cutters. It won't dull the blade, and protects the table or counter you're working on. Don't use your rotary cutter on any surface other than a rotary-cutting mat, or it will ruin the blade as well as the surface on which you're cutting.

Most mats come with grid lines and other markings on them. These markings are best for rough cutting, not precision cutting. Mats come in many sizes, colors, and shapes with special features for a variety of uses. For basic cutting, a 24" x 36" mat works well. At a minimum, an 18" x 24" mat will do if you don't have room for a larger size.

! Problem Solving

Don't place hot objects such as coffee mugs or irons on your cutting mat, because the high temperatures will warp the mat. Cold temperatures can make mats brittle and easy to break. Store your mats flat and away from temperature extremes.

Rotary-Cutting Rulers

Rotary-cutting rulers are generally precision cut from ⅛"-thick clear acrylic. Markings are printed on the bottom surface of the ruler for accurate visibility from the top. You'll find many other design features, including various edge shadings, angled interior lines, non-skid features, lips and edges, and so on. The options are vast. If you can imagine it, it's probably available.

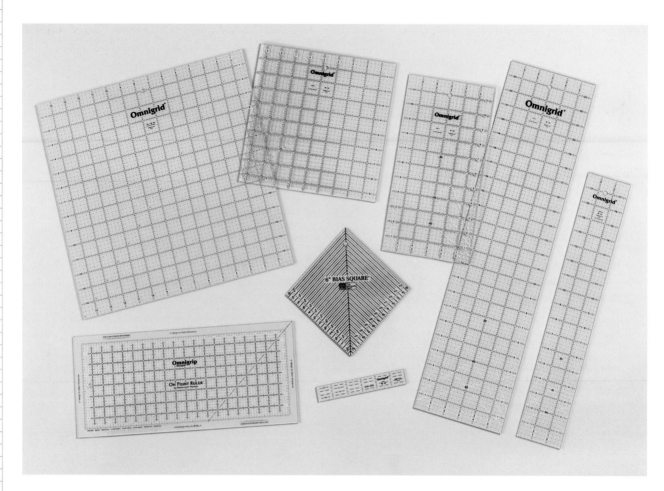

An assortment of rulers is nice to have for cutting and measuring.

While rotary-cutting rulers are available for just about any purpose you can imagine, let's deal with the simple basics that will give you the most versatility in measuring and cutting shapes and dimensions.

When selecting rulers, look for the following features:

- Be made of ⅛"-thick hard acrylic.

- Have a "window" at the inch intersections to help you see to better align the marks with the fabric edges.

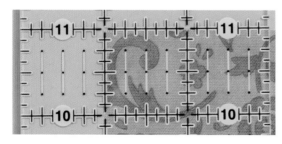

- Include 1" grids and ⅛" increments marked on the grid lines. The more ⅛" lines that are connected, the better your ability to measure precisely. My favorite ruler has an allover ⅛" grid. It's like working with transparent graph paper.

? Did You Know?

Why do you need a minimum of a 12"-long ruler? A basic ruler needs to be long enough to span at least 11" of fabric width (44"-wide fabric folded into four layers) in order for you to cut strips.

Your basic ruler inventory should include the following:

- A 6" x 12" or 6" x 24" ruler is essential. Both sizes are nice but you need only one if you must choose. Purchase a ruler with 30°-, 45°-, and 60°-angle lines, which are helpful for cutting various diamonds and equilateral triangles

- It's nice to have an assortment of square rulers. A 15" or larger square ruler is very useful for cutting wide borders, squaring up quilt corners, or trimming large blocks. A smaller 6" or 8" ruler with a diagonal line running from corner to corner and a ⅛" gridded corner is handy for trimming half-square-triangle units or smaller blocks and patch units.

- A 1" x 6" ruler isn't essential but is handy to keep by your sewing machine to check the accuracy of your piecing as you work or run into problems.

- At some point you'll want to buy an Omnigrid On-Point Ruler. Standard rotary-cutting rulers measure squares and other right-angle shapes from side to side. Many quilts have pieced borders or blocks with on-point patchwork units that need to measure evenly across their diagonals in order to fit in the block. This ruler allows you to cut those diagonal measurements.

Basic Cutting

The most frequently cut shapes in patchwork are squares, rectangles, and two types of right triangles—half-square triangles and quarter-square triangles. All of these shapes are cut from strips of fabric that have been cut to specific widths.

Before you can make your first cut, you must prepare your fabric by pressing it and refolding it selvage to selvage. Unless you have a 24"-long ruler, fold the fabric a second time from fold to selvages as

shown below. Make sure all the layers are pressed smooth and flat with no creases or misalignments at the folded edge(s).

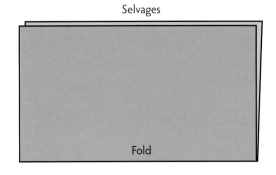

Selvages

Fold

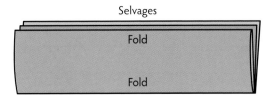

Selvages

Fold

Fold

Creating a Clean-Cut Edge

Before cutting, you'll need a clean-cut edge from which to cut strips. This edge must be at a right angle to the fold, or the strips you eventually cut will have dog legs, or Vs, at the folds when opened up to their full length. This two-ruler method ensures a good right-angle cut and sets you up for cutting your first strip without having to rotate your cutting mat or, even worse, to move your fabric, which can shift layers.

1. Arrange your pressed and folded fabric on your cutting mat with the folds closest to you and the selvages away from you. If you're right-handed, you'll always work from left to right. If you're left-handed, you'll work from right to left.

> ## ! Problem Solving
>
> If you're left-handed, visual instructions and diagrams can be confusing because they're often presented by, or for, right-handed quilters. When working with a book or pattern presenting a right-handed diagram, use a mirror to see the left-handed version.
>
> When watching a live demonstration of a skill, place yourself in front of the instructor face to face. You'll be seeing the mirror-image, left-handed version of the demonstration. Right-handed quilters should always stand behind a demonstrator, looking over her shoulder, to see things from the correct perspective.

2. Place your 12"- or 24"-long ruler over the ragged edges of the fabric so that they're completely covered. To make a cut at a right angle to the fold, place one edge of a square ruler along the fold of

the fabric and adjust the long ruler so it's flush with the square ruler.

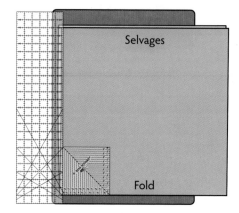

Right-handed cutting

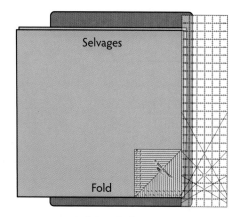

Left-handed cutting

3. Hold the long ruler in place with firm, downward pressure and your hand flat with fingers splayed wide to help stabilize the ruler. Use your body weight, pressing from the shoulder to exert downward pressure, which will prevent muscle fatigue in your hands. Some quilters find it helpful to anchor their outer fingers off the ruler on the side away from the cutting. Keep any fingers on the ruler away from the cutting edges. You want to keep those fingertips!

4. While still holding the ruler, move the square ruler out of the way, pick up your cutter, and release the safety to expose the blade. Placing the blade next to the ruler edge and holding your cutter at a comfortable 45° angle, begin cutting slowly from below the folds away from yourself toward the selvages. Cut completely past the

selvages and engage the safety mechanism before putting the cutter down. **Note:** Some people prefer to place their index finger on the etched ridge on the cutter for extra control and comfort. Some, like myself, find that position awkward. Try both finger positions and see what works best for you.

5. Without moving or shifting your fabric at all, lift the long ruler and remove the ragged edges you just trimmed away. You now have a clean-cut edge from which to begin cutting strips.

Cutting Strips

The most basic unit of rotary cutting is a strip. From strips you can crosscut squares, rectangles, shorter strips, and subsequently other shapes, so it's very important to learn how to cut strips accurately.

1. Align the ruler so that the measurement of the strip width you wish to cut is along the length of the clean-cut edge. At the same time, align a horizontal ruler line along the folds on the bottom. This helps ensure that each cut is a right-angle cut.

! Problem Solving

Any time you can't match both horizontal and vertical lines of the ruler on the cut edge of the fabric, it's time to make a new clean-cut edge.

2. With the ruler carefully aligned, release the safety mechanism on the cutter and cut away from your body, running the blade of the cutter along the

ruler edge completely across the selvages at the top. Engage the safety mechanism.

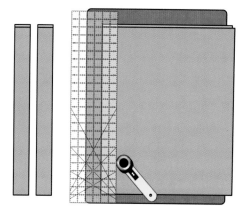

3. Carefully move the strip away from the body of fabric and proceed to cut as many more strips as needed. Try not to move the main piece of fabric until absolutely necessary. As soon as you move it, you're likely to misalign the fabric edges, and you may need to make a new clean-cut edge.

4. Before using the strips further, cut the selvages from the ends. Align the ruler with the long cut edge of the strip and trim away the selvages with a right-angle cut.

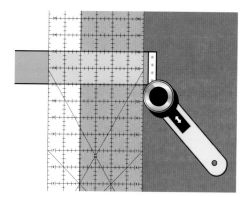

! Problem Solving

Many quilters wonder where to line up their fabric edge in relation to the thickness of the ruler line. The answer is to straddle the line. This is where those "windows" at the 1" grid intersections on a ruler can be very helpful. You can see exactly where the fabric edge is placed in relation to the line.

Cutting Squares

Cut squares from strips of fabric. To determine the width of the strip, add ½" to the desired finished size of the square.

1. Cut strips the width of the cut square (finished size + ½"). Remove the selvages.

2. Turn the strip so the length is running from left to right in front of you. Using your rotary ruler, measure the same width as the strip, also placing a ruler line on the long edge of the strip to ensure a right-angle cut. Crosscut the strip into squares. If at any time you can't align the long edge with a ruler line, stop and trim the short edge of the strip to a right-angle cut.

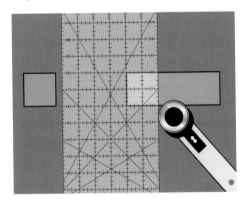

? Did You Know?

The word *crosscut* is used frequently in quiltmaking patterns and instructions. It means to cut across a strip or strip set to make squares and rectangles.

Cutting Rectangles

Rectangles are also cut from strips. Cut the strip width to either the long dimension or the short dimension. Usually the choice is made based on the most efficient way to cut rectangles from the selvage-to-selvage length. However, design considerations, such as the best use of a directional print or stripe, can also come into play. Just as with squares, add ½" to both finished dimensions of the rectangle to get your cut size. Cut the strips the width of one of those dimensions. Crosscut the strips into rectangles using the second dimension.

For example, to cut rectangles that will finish to 2" x 4", add ½" to both dimensions to determine the cut size of the rectangle. In this case, that would be 2½" x 4½".

1. Cut strips 2½" wide.

2. Turn the strip and crosscut rectangles 4½" long.

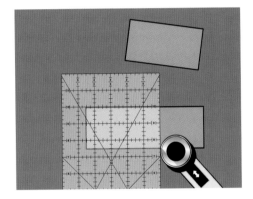

? Did You Know?

A square is a kind of rectangle. A rectangle has two pairs of parallel sides and four 90° corners. On a rectangle, the opposite sides are the same length, but one pair is shorter than the other. A square is actually a rectangle having all four sides of the same length.

Cutting Right Triangles

Quilters use two types of right triangles in piecing—half-square and quarter-square triangles. Both types start with a square, as their names imply. Create half-square triangles and quarter-square triangles by cutting squares in half diagonally or into quarters diagonally. Which type of triangle you use is determined by where you want the straight of grain to lie on your triangle.

Half-square triangles. You can make two half-square triangles by cutting a square diagonally from corner to corner. The grain line of both triangles will lie on the two short legs with the bias on the long edge.

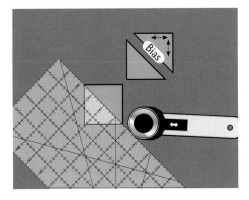

To calculate the size of the parent square, add ⅞" to the finished length of the short leg of the triangle. Cut a square this size, and then cut it in half diagonally to yield two triangles. Once sewn into place in a block or pieced unit, the triangles will measure the desired finished size along their short legs.

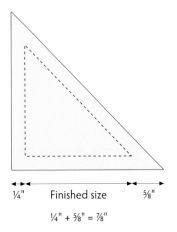

¼"   Finished size   ⅝"

¼" + ⅝" = ⅞"

Quarter-square triangles. You can make four quarter-square triangles by cutting a square diagonally into quarters. The straight-grain line of the four triangles will lie on the long edges, and the bias will be on the short legs.

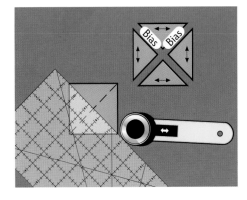

There are three "magic numbers" you need to know in quiltmaking: ½", ⅞", and 1¼".

- Add ½" to the finished dimensions (for seam allowances) to determine cut sizes of all squares, rectangles, or strips.

- Add ⅞" to the finished dimension of the short side of a right triangle to determine the cut size of a square to be cut into half-square triangles.

- Add 1¼" to the finished dimension of the long side of a right triangle to determine the cut size of a square to be cut into quarter-square triangles.

Even if you don't intend to plan your own blocks and cutting sizes, there are often times when using commercial patterns that you'll want to determine the finished sizes of pieces. You can do this if you know how much was added for cut sizes.

For example, let's say you cut 2⅞" squares, and then cut them in half on the diagonal. You can determine the finished size of those triangles by subtracting ⅞" from what you cut. Voilà! The triangles will finish to 2". If you do that with all the pieces in a block, you can determine the finished size of the entire block as well, and that's important information to have.

To calculate the size square to start with, add 1¼" to the finished length of the long edge of the triangle. Cut a square this size and cut it into quarters diagonally to yield four triangles. Once sewn into place in a block or unit, the triangles will measure the desired finished size along their long edges.

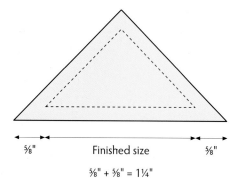

5⁄8"   Finished size   5⁄8"

5⁄8" + 5⁄8" = 1¼"

Cutting Other Shapes

Besides the frequently used common shapes already discussed, there are often other shapes you'll need to rotary cut. Here are a few shapes you may encounter in quiltmaking.

Equilateral Triangle

Equilateral triangles have three equal-length sides and 60° angles at the corners. They are easy to cut using the 60°-angle line on your regular rotary-cutting ruler. (Ideally, it's easiest to use a ruler with two intersecting 60° lines as shown in the illustrations.) Start by cutting straight-grain strips ¾" larger than the height of your triangle.

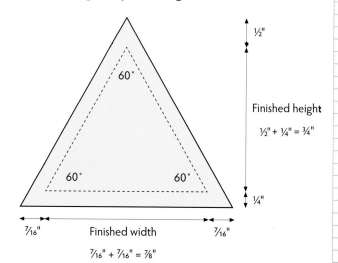

½"

Finished height

½" + ¼" = ¾"

¼"

60°

60°   60°

7⁄16"   Finished width   7⁄16"

7⁄16" + 7⁄16" = ⅞"

Right-handed cutting:

1. Place the 60°-angle line on the upper edge of the strip, intersecting the upper-right corner. Make the first cut.

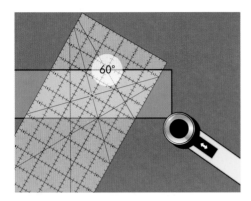

2. Pivot—don't lift—the ruler clockwise so the other 60° line is now on the lower edge of the strip exactly at the point of the first cut. Make the second cut.

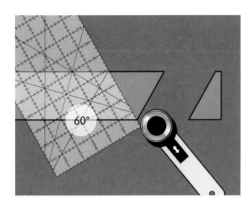

3. Continue cutting triangles from the length of your strip in the same fashion.

Left-handed cutting:

1. Place the 60°-angle line on the upper edge of the strip, intersecting the corner. Make the first cut.

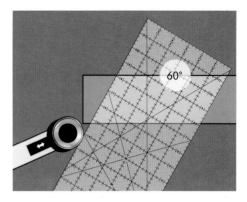

2. Pivot—don't lift—the ruler clockwise so the other 60° line is now on the upper edge of the strip exactly at the point of the first cut. Make the second cut.

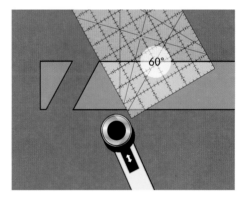

3. Continue cutting triangles from the length of your strip in the same fashion.

Half-Rectangle Triangles

Create half-rectangle triangles by cutting rectangles in half diagonally. Note that cutting on opposite diagonals results in mirror-image triangles.

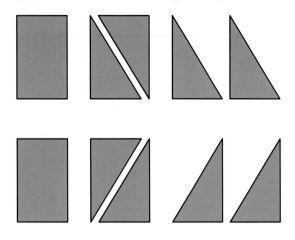

The math for cutting this type of triangle doesn't often result in even ⅛" dimensions, so I find it most accurate to use a paper cutting guide (page 29) to cut the parent rectangles from fabric strips.

1. On graph paper, draw the desired half-rectangle triangle. Add ¼" seam allowance to all three sides.

2. Square off and finish the triangle, with seam allowances included, into a full rectangle.

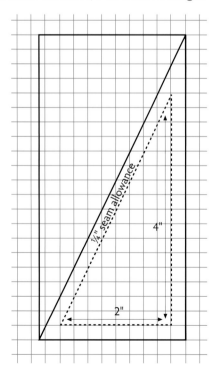

3. Refer to "Paper Cutting Guides" to make a paper rectangle guide to cut strips. Crosscut the strips into rectangles.

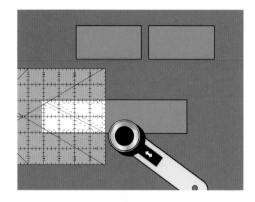

4. Cut each rectangle in half diagonally to make two triangles, being careful to cut on the correct diagonal.

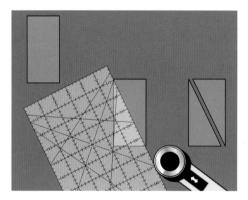

Diamonds and Parallelograms

A parallelogram is a four-sided shape with two pairs of parallel sides. The opposite sides are of equal length, and the opposite angles are also the same size. Think of it as a tilted rectangle.

A diamond is a type of parallelogram with *four* sides of equal length. Opposite angles are of equal measure but not 90° like a square. Think of them as squares tilted to the side. The three most frequently used diamonds in quiltmaking are called 30°, 45°, and 60° diamonds.

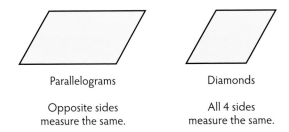

Parallelograms	Diamonds
Opposite sides measure the same.	All 4 sides measure the same.

If you're working from your own design, you'll need a full-sized accurate drawing of your diamond or parallelogram on good-quality graph paper. There are two or three possible ways to cut diamonds and parallelograms. All methods are not necessarily appropriate for all diamonds and parallelograms.

The first is to make a paper cutting guide (page 29). This method works for diamonds or parallelograms of any size. It's particularly useful for instances when the height of a 30° or 60° diamond or parallelogram doesn't measure in even ⅛" increments.

The second method is to cut straight-grain strips of fabric and use the 45°- or 60°-angle lines on a regular rotary-cutting ruler to crosscut the diamonds or parallelograms. This method works when the height of your diamond is an even ⅛" measurement.

In addition, you can use the On-Point Ruler to cut 45° diamonds or parallelograms. In this case, all you need to know is the finished length of the sides. There is no math and no need to add anything for seam allowances. The On-Point Ruler does not work for 30° or 60° shapes.

Method 1

1. Make a full-sized drawing of your unit on graph paper. Add ¼" seam allowances on all four sides.

2. Refer to "Paper Cutting Guides" to make two cutting guides of the diamond and tape them to your regular rotary-cutting ruler.

3. Cut strips the width of the paper cutting guides.

4. Turn the strip and crosscut diamonds from the length of it.

Method 2

1. Cut strips ½" larger than the height of your unit.

2. For 30° diamonds, add 1" to the finished length of the side. For 45° diamonds, add ¾"; for 60° diamonds, add ⅝".

30° diamond

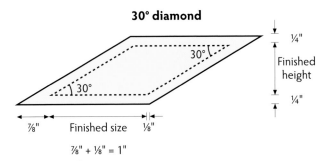

45° diamond

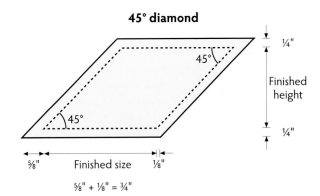

60° diamond

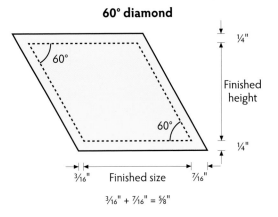

3. Using the calculation from step 2, mark increments along the edge of the strip.

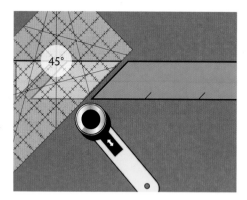

4. Crosscut diamonds using the corresponding 30°-, 45°-, or 60°-angle line on your ruler.

Method 3

For 45° diamonds, you can use the On-Point Ruler to cut diamonds without any math at all. The only thing you need to know is the finished length of the side.

1. Using the On-Point Ruler, cut strips using the ruler mark equal to the finished side length of the diamond. For instance, if the finished side length is 4", cut strips using the 4" mark of the On-Point Ruler.

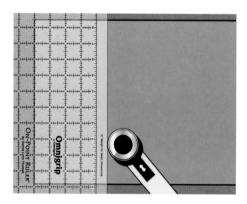

2. Place the diagonal line on the corner of the ruler on the top edge of the strip as shown. If you're left-handed, you'll start from the opposite corner. Trim the corner of the strip at a 45° angle.

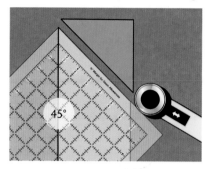

Right-handed cutting

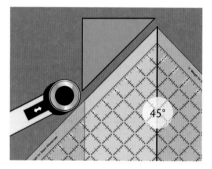

Left-handed cutting

3. Turn the strip and place the corner diagonal line of the ruler back on the top of the strip. Cut diamonds from the strip length using the same 4" mark.

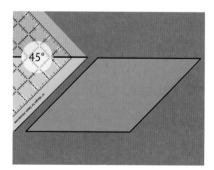

Right-handed cutting

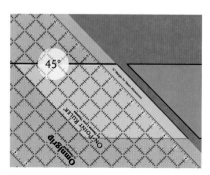

Left-handed cutting

Paper Cutting Guides

Sometimes a quilt requires an odd shape that doesn't measure evenly in ⅛" increments, making a standard rotary-cutting ruler difficult to use. In situations such as this, it's helpful to make paper cutting guides.

1. Begin with an accurate full-sized drawing of the shape you need to cut. Draw ¼" seam allowances on all four sides. Trace this shape onto a translucent tracing paper or even freezer paper. Make two. Cut out the guides and tape them to the underside of your ruler with the guides' edges aligned with the ruler's edge. Spread the templates far enough apart to give enough distance to cut an accurate strip length.

2. Cut strips the width of the guides.

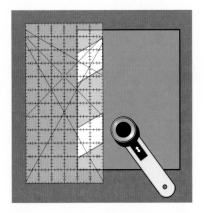

3. Turn the strip and crosscut the second dimension using the other edge of the guide. In some cases it may be necessary to reposition the guide on the ruler so that you can cut the units from the strip. Remember, the side of the cutting guide that you want to cut must be the side aligned with the edge of the ruler.

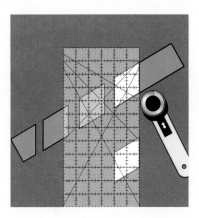

Cutting Diagonal Measurements with the On-Point Ruler

Regular rotary-cutting rulers cut shapes that measure evenly from side to side. But sometimes you need pieces that measure evenly across their diagonals in order to be set on point inside borders or other straight-set patchwork units.

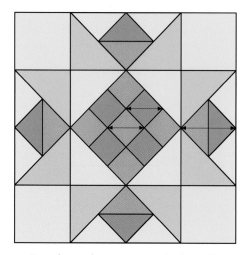

Even diagonal measurements (indicated by arrows) are needed for the squares in the center nine patch and half-square-triangle units on each side.

You can use the Omnigrid On-Point Ruler to cut squares, rectangles, and half-square triangles, as well as to cut and sew strip sets and segments for strip piecing. All of this is done in the same way you would use a regular rotary-cutting ruler. Although it looks like a regular rotary-cutting ruler, the On-Point Ruler is not interchangeable with regular rulers because its marked measurements are different.

Squares

In order to cut squares that measure evenly across the diagonal, first decide what you want the diagonal of the square to measure when finished. Cut strips using that mark on the Omnigrid On-Point Ruler.

There's nothing to add to the desired finished diagonal size, even for seam allowances. The ruler has a ½" margin around all four edges that accommodates the two ¼" seam allowances on all right-angle units.

2" finished

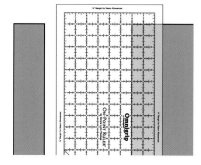

Desired diagonal measurement = ruler cutting mark

Rectangles

Just as with squares, there's no math involved in cutting rectangles that will be set on point with even diagonal measurements. Unlike squares, though, there are two diagonals to measure and cut: the short diagonal and the long diagonal.

The simplest way to determine the size to cut is to make a full-scale drawing of the block with the rectangle. Lay the marked part of the ruler (do not include the clear margin edge) on the unit and measure it. Cut strips using the indicated mark for the short cut, and then crosscut rectangles from the strip using the long mark.

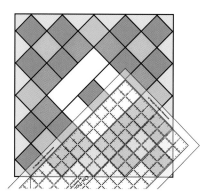

If you don't have a full-sized drawing of the block, you can still calculate the cutting marks if you know the desired diagonal sizes of the other units in the block. In reality, you determine those sizes for yourself, depending on what size you want the block to be.

Look at the Album block in the diagram below. I want the block to be 10" finished. That means each of the five small squares across the top of the block must measure 2" diagonally. Therefore, the short diagonal of the rectangle is also the same size as the small squares.

Follow these steps to determine the long cut of the rectangle.

1. "Square off" the corner of the rectangle as shown by the red lines.

2. The long cut is twice the measurement of one red line.

To find the length of one of the red lines, begin with the diagonal measurement of the squares, which we already decided would be 2" in the 10" block. The red line runs across the diagonal of 1½ squares. Because each square is 2" on the diagonal, then the diagonal of 1½ squares is 3" (2 x 1½ = 3). Double this number and you have the cutting mark for the long side of the rectangle (6" mark).

To summarize, cut the rectangles from strips using the 2" mark, and then crosscut into rectangles using the 6" mark. This process works in the same way for all rectangles.

Half-Square Triangles

To cut half-square triangles that measure evenly on the diagonal, add ½" to the desired diagonal measurement of the long edge. Cut strips using this mark and crosscut them into squares using the same mark. Cut the squares in half diagonally to create half-square triangles. When sewn in place, the triangles will measure the desired diagonal width.

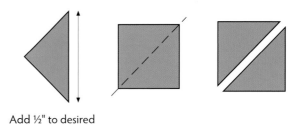

Add ½" to desired diagonal measurement.

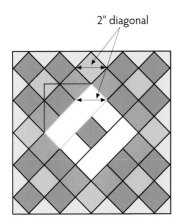

2" diagonal

"Make Me Smile," pieced by Donna Lynn Thomas and quilted by Denise Mariano, from *On-Point Patchwork*

Pressing

Pressing is an important subject that's often neglected. Although the equipment need not be fancy or expensive, there are important skills and considerations to master in order for your blocks and intersections to match and lie flat.

Equipment

All you need are a reliable iron that has a setting for cotton, an ironing surface, and some ironing sprays.

Irons

Many people prefer a steam iron, but steam isn't necessary as you can replace steam with a good spray water bottle that emits a fine mist. Others don't want the steam function, because many irons tend to spit and leak from the steam vents. There's always much discussion about the perfect iron when quilters gather. Iron features change frequently so keep your ear out for word-of-mouth recommendations.

Another feature that some like and others don't is an automatic shut-off. Some quilters like them to prevent an accident. Others look for irons *without* this function because they leave their irons on for a long period of time and tire of "shaking it awake" after 10 minutes of nonuse.

Whichever iron you use, keep the soleplate clean and free from adhesives, starches, or other chemicals by cleaning it periodically with an iron-cleaning solution. Don't leave water in the tank of a steam iron for long periods and periodically descale the iron if tap water is used. All of these instructions should be in the owner's manual.

Ironing Surfaces

You can iron on a variety of surfaces—from a travel-sized roll-up mat, to a tabletop board, to a professional-grade floor-standing model, to a custom over-sized ironing board made just for quilters. Make sure any freestanding ironing board you use is sturdy and won't easily tip over.

The most important feature of any ironing surface is that it be firm, not soft. A firm surface will help you produce sharper seams. Keep your ironing surface clean, and replace the cover as necessary to avoid damage to your iron's soleplate. Use a protective cover on the surface when working with adhesives or other damaging chemicals. Never leave your iron face down on the ironing surface, or you may find your board scorched or, worse, on fire.

Sprays

Many quilters swear by starch for controlling fabric and creating sharp creases. Others don't like it because of the starch buildup on the iron, rotary blades, and sewing-machine needles. Some quilters, like me, prefer a starch-free spray to ensure a sharp, crisp seam without the gunky buildup from starch. Again, these are all personal choices.

I use a mix of steam from the iron, dry iron, starch alternatives, and water spray to work with my seams, depending on pressing needs, as I'll discuss next.

How to Press

It's important to get all the wrinkles out of your fabric before cutting, so make sure all the folded fabric layers are pressed smooth and wrinkle-free. Use steam in your iron and a starch alternative or water spray, if necessary. The steam, while really helping to eliminate wrinkles, also helps cotton "stick" to itself. This is a nice plus if you'll be cutting right after pressing. Layers don't shift as easily if they've recently been steamed.

 Blue-Ribbon Skills

If you press out a deep wrinkle *after* a strip is cut, it can change the size or shape of the strip. If this has happened, it's best to go back and cut the strip or unit again to make sure it's accurate.

Pressing a seam is the gentle lowering, pressing, and lifting of the iron along the length of a seam. Don't be aggressive as this can easily distort the bias and crosswise-grain edges or seams in your pieced unit.

Pressing to One Side

A properly pressed seam is pressed to one side, without any pleats, distortions, or puckering on the right side. Here are a few tips to ensure good pressing results.

- Always press the seam line flat after sewing, before pressing the seam allowances in one direction or the other, to set the thread. By setting the thread you help it relax into the weave of the fabric, making for a noticeably smoother and finer turn. In addition, setting the thread can help alleviate any minor thread tension problems. Major tension problems must be dealt with by correcting the problem with the sewing machine.

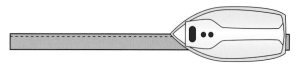

- Press your fabric *over* the seam allowances, working from the right side. Nudge the top piece over the seam allowances, avoiding any back-and-forth or aggressive motion. You'll have much better results working from the front than trying to manipulate a small ¼"-wide piece of fabric with a big iron on the wrong side. By working with the wrong side of the unit against the ironing surface, the narrow seam allowance is held stabilized in place where you want it. The result of working from the back, instead of the front, is often a pleat or incompletely opened seam when you turn it over.

- Use a dry iron on the cotton setting when nudging the seam allowances in place. Too much moisture at this point in the process can distort the bias and crosswise grains. Once the seam is pressed in place, use a starch alternative or water spray to sharpen the crease. Don't use any back-and-forth motion while the fabric is damp. Simply press the seam and lift, letting the heat and moisture do the work for you. A rounded seam isn't a well-pressed seam, as it won't always accurately reflect the true size of the patchwork unit or strip set until later when, with repeated pressing during the assembly process, it finally flattens out.

- Always press each seam after you sew it and before adding another strip to a strip set or crossing one seam with another. Unpressed strip sets are a mess to try to press all at once, causing grain line stretching in the process. Unpressed crossing seams can also be problematic. When you do get around to pressing them, you'll find it's common for pleats to form or for points to be lopped off in the unpressed folds. Pressing as you go is an extra step worth doing to maintain accuracy. Besides, it's good for you to get up and down repeatedly to go iron instead of sitting for hours! Your circulation will love you for it.

- When pressing crosswise-grain strip sets and bias-edge seams, always move the iron in the direction of the straight of grain. This will help prevent stretching. Don't use steam or moisture until the seam is in place.

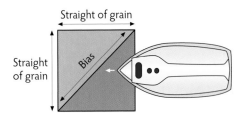

Straight of grain

Straight of grain

Bias

! Problem Solving

When you've mistakenly pressed seam allowances in the wrong direction, don't try to re-press them directly from the wrong direction to the correct direction. First, you need to remove the original incorrect crease, or the fabric won't turn to the new position without a fight. To do this, arrange the pieced seam in its original unpressed position. Spray the seam with water and press it flat, removing the original crease completely. Press until the moisture is gone. Once the original crease is completely eliminated, you can press in the new direction without difficulty.

Pressing Open—or Not

Unlike in garment construction, quilters generally don't press seam allowances open, although it's becoming more common to find instructions telling you to do that. While you may not give it a thought, there are several good reasons why it *isn't* the best solution.

- You must closely match your thread color, because the threads can easily be quite visible when suspended between the two pieces of fabric.

- Unless you're working with very simple piecing, you'll have a buildup of overlapping seam allowances at intersections. Seam allowances are better dispersed when pressed to one side.

- Nesting seam allowances is the main way we have of making tightly matched intersections without having to pin every single seam. Despite the pinning issue, intersections and points are more perfect when seam allowances are nested.

- Pressing seam allowances open is more tedious and time consuming because you must work to manipulate tiny little seam allowances from the back of your piece. It's quicker and tidier to work from the right side, pressing the top fabric over the seam allowances, which are secured against the ironing surface. You're also less likely to create pleats when working from the front of the fabric.

- The batting is more likely to sneak out of seam allowances that have been pressed open, whereas there's no opening for it to escape from when the seam allowances have been pressed to one side.

Which Way to Press

To this day you still hear the rule of thumb stating to "press seam allowances toward the darker fabric." But think about it, what if all the pieces are dark? What if all the dark pieces at an intersection converge on each other? In reality, this rule of thumb is a last consideration after two more-important pressing goals are met.

> **? Did You Know?**
>
> **The idea to press** toward the dark fabric came from the desire to avoid shadowing of dark fabrics through lighter ones. Shadowing was more of an issue with old-time, poor-quality, loosely woven fabrics, not with our contemporary quilter's cotton.

Goals for Good Pressing

The first goal of pressing is to evenly distribute the bulk of many seam allowances meeting at an intersection. The second goal is to "butt" or "nest" the seam ridges so that they form tight intersections. Usually in order to attend to the first, you'll need to do the second. The two goals are interdependent.

By nesting the ridges of seam allowances that meet, you naturally distribute bulk evenly across the area. Bulky junctions are difficult for a sewing-machine presser foot to navigate, often resulting in inaccuracies, along with a great deal of frustration on your part. But by nesting seam ridges, you also create seams that abut tightly against each other, matching exactly to form sharp, perfect points. You also eliminate the need to pin every intersection, letting the nesting do the job for you in most cases.

It's just as important to nest diagonal seams at an intersection as it is to nest straight seams. Care must be taken to ensure that all the seams that meet anywhere in a block or from block to block be pressed in opposite directions. It's not as difficult to do as you think, and with practice you get pretty good at it.

Making a Pressing Plan

Before you head out on a cross-country car trip, or sometimes even before a trip across town, you plan how you're going to get there. (Well, most of us do!) The same is true for planning where you want your seam allowances to lie before you take a stitch. By making a pressing plan, you'll know which way to press each seam allowance every step of the way. By distributing bulk and nesting seam ridges, you eliminate the need to rip and re-press seams that you discover should have been pressed in the opposite direction.

Making a pressing plan is not a difficult thing to do unless you're dealing with very complex blocks. Begin by making a drawing of your block. It doesn't have to be fancy—a sketch will do. It just needs to accurately represent where the seams meet. If the blocks will be set together without sashing, then you need to draw more blocks abutting the sides of the first block so you can see where seams might meet.

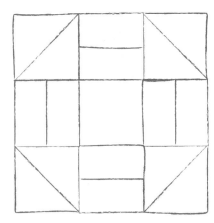

Once the blocks are sketched out, trace over them in ink. Now, working with a pencil, begin working out pressing directions using arrows on each seam. If blocks are going to be set together with sashing, then you can usually work your pressing from the center outward.

If the blocks are to be sewn together without sashing, then the seams where the blocks meet is the first place to start. What happens on the edge of the block affects the interior, so you want to start at the edge and work your way in toward the center.

Following are a few rules of thumb to keep in mind as you work.

Don't press all sides of a patch toward its center. This creates too much bulk behind one piece. This is especially true for triangles.

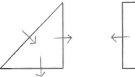

Press away from the center of the block, dispersing seam allowances out toward the edges, unless there's a compelling reason to do otherwise.

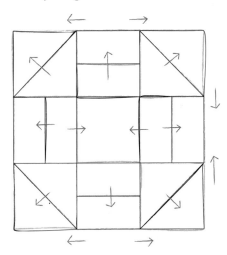

Nine-patch and four-patch constructions are easy to plan. In this diagram, option A presses all the seam allowances in opposite directions from row to row. Option B presses all seam allowances "in and out" alternately from row to row. Both plans are fine for blocks with sashing.

Some blocks are conducive to circular pressing. Press all seam allowances in either a consistent clockwise or counterclockwise direction. Release a few stitches in the center where all the seams meet in order to facilitate the circular pressing.

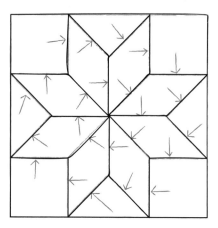

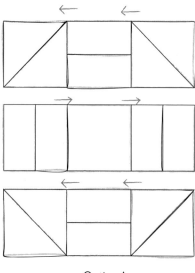

Option A

Option B

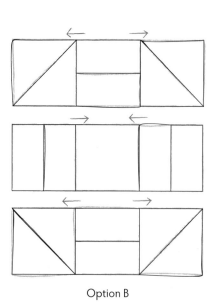

Blue-Ribbon Skills

Rather than using a seam ripper to release a few stitches in the center of a unit you want to press circularly, use your fingers to do what I call the "four-patch pop."

Fold the two sides of the seam allowance in the direction you want them to go using the thumbs on each hand.

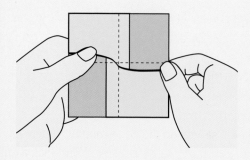

A quick pop and twist will release those stitches, allowing the seam allowances to move freely.

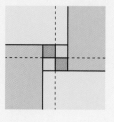

Plan your pressing so that diagonal seams that meet to form a point are pressed in opposite directions. It's a sure guarantee of sharp points.

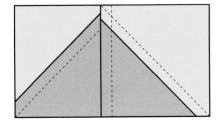

Create a flow from one side of a unit to the other. Look at how the seam allowances inside the alternating pieced flying-geese units flow from one side to the other. By alternating the directional flow from one unit to the next, the center seams nest and the change in flow from left to right ensures there isn't too much bulk pressed behind each triangle.

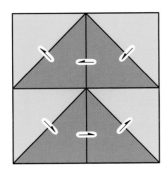

Consider how your blocks will be set together when planning your pressing. If you'll be setting blocks together without sashing or in a nine-patch type of construction, pressing option B shown on page 38 is a better choice. By pressing the final two seams joining the rows toward the center of the block, you can nest seams on the edges neatly. When sewing the blocks together, turn every other block a quarter turn so the side seams nest with the top- and bottom-row seams.

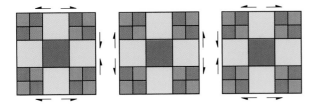

Press in the opposite direction. Sometimes it may be best to press the seam allowances at two opposite corners of a block in the reverse direction from the other two opposite corners when the blocks are going to be set together side by side without sashing. The seams at the corner will now nest when the blocks are sewn together.

Circular pressing works for block-to-block sewing. Seams will nest nicely at intersections because what is pressed upward on one block will always be pressed downward on the next. Circular pressing only works if all the blocks are pressed in the same circular direction—either clockwise or counterclockwise. Do this with any block that has a central point, such as four-patch block construction and star blocks like the LeMoyne Star shown below.

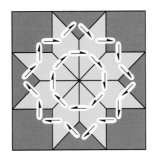

Flip if you must! I am not beyond flipping the direction of seam allowances in the middle so that one end is facing one way and the other end is facing the opposite way. In this way, both intersections that the seam crosses can nest. A snip in the middle helps the seam allowances lie flat. This is an option of last resort, but in complex piecing it can be useful.

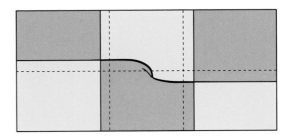

"Pineapple Fizz," pieced and quilted by Jeanne Zyck, from *Patchwork Palette*

Block Construction

efore you can start sewing, you need to understand how your block will be put together. If you're working with a commercial pattern, this will be described for you. Even so, it's a good idea to review the pattern first so you understand where you're going.

For projects you design on your own, it's important to understand the assembly process, and to do that you need to see how your block breaks apart. Most traditional blocks follow a simple three-step process: individual pieces are joined into units, units are joined into larger units or rows, and rows are joined to make blocks.

It's quite common to see the phrase four-patch, nine-patch, or five-patch construction used. "Patch" does not necessarily indicate the number of pieces in a block, but rather how the final pieced units or individual pieces are sewn together to finish the block.

In the illustrations that follow, the dark lines indicate the final seams to be sewn to create the blocks, often breaking the block apart into the number of units that correspond to the four-patch, five-patch, or nine-patch construction.

> ## ? Did You Know?
>
> **The term *finished* size** refers to the finished size of a block after all seams have been sewn, including those on the edges. The *cut size* is the size of the block including the ¼" seam allowances on the edges. The finished size is always ½" smaller than the cut size.

Four-Patch Construction

Let's look at some four-patch block constructions. In many cases individual pieces are joined to make a larger patch or unit. Blocks such as this may actually have as many as 16 or more individual pieces in their breakdown, but the block is still called a Four Patch block if those smaller pieces can be assembled into four larger units, which are then sewn together to complete the block.

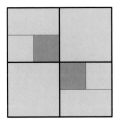 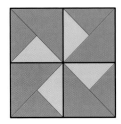

Oftentimes there are multiple ways to assemble the same block. Instead of making four final units, the block can be broken into rows and sewn together row by row. Sometimes I choose one method over the other if I require a certain pressing pattern such as circular or in and out.

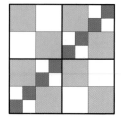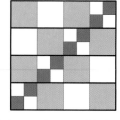

This is an example of a block that can be assembled in units (left) or rows (right).

No matter how simple or complex the block, always begin with the individual pieces sewn into units. Sew those units into rows or larger units. Then finish the block by sewing the units or rows together.

Nine-Patch Construction

Nine-patch construction is very much like four-patch construction except there are three rows of three pieces or units. Each unit may be lightly or heavily pieced, but as long as the final construction is 3 x 3, it's a nine-patch construction. Here are some examples of nine-patch construction.

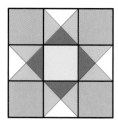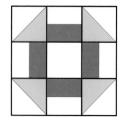

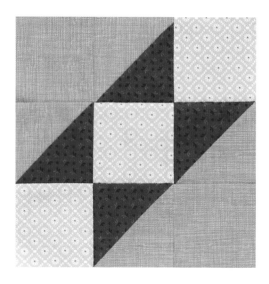

Five-Patch Construction

Take a look at some examples of five-patch construction. As always, "patches" can refer to individual pieces or pieced units that will be assembled into the block.

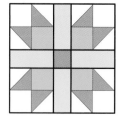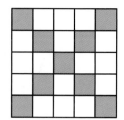

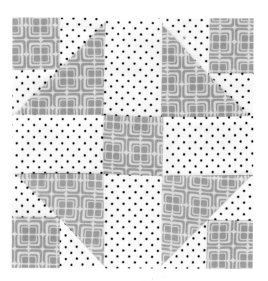

Circular Construction

People often identify circular construction with eight-pointed or six-pointed stars. That's true, but there are other blocks that don't look like stars that also use circular construction. Take a look at some examples of circular construction.

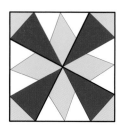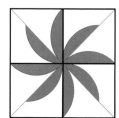

Eccentric Construction

Eccentric construction doesn't fit neatly into any of the previous categories. Often this type of block must be sewn with a partial-seam technique because the final seams don't run completely across the block from one side to the other (see "Partial Seams" on page 60).

Here are two examples of eccentric block construction.

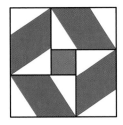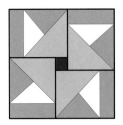

Diagonal Construction

Many quilt blocks are assembled in diagonal rows. Diagonally assembled blocks are marked by the presence of quarter-square and half-square triangles on the edges of the blocks to make them square.

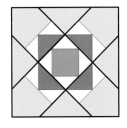

"Gems," pieced by Donna Lynn Thomas and quilted by Denise Mariano, from *Patchwork Palette*

Machine Piecing

While some quilters still hand piece, most are introduced to the art of quilt-making using their sewing machines exclusively. It's our most important and expensive tool, and although there are many advanced skills and techniques for machine piecing, mastering the basics is still of primary importance. If you learn to use your machine well to produce consistent, accurate results, you'll have many happy years of frustration-free piecing.

The Sewing Machine

The most important piece of equipment for machine piecing is your sewing machine. It doesn't need to be fancy; all that's necessary is a machine that stitches forward and backward with a fine-quality straight stitch. Like any piece of equipment, it should be properly maintained, and you should be familiar with its parts and operation. Read and refer to your owner's manual frequently to learn how to oil, clean, troubleshoot, and maintain your machine. Have your machine professionally cleaned and serviced at least yearly. In addition, many modern computerized machines often need software updates, sometimes more than once a year. Check with your dealer periodically for information on any available updates. There's a lot of information available online, including instructional tutorials, sewing-machine user forums, and even replacement manuals for older machines. Make use of these resources, no matter the age or complexity of your machine.

If you clean and oil your machine according to your owner's manual every time you start a new quilt, you'll find your machine will run happily for many

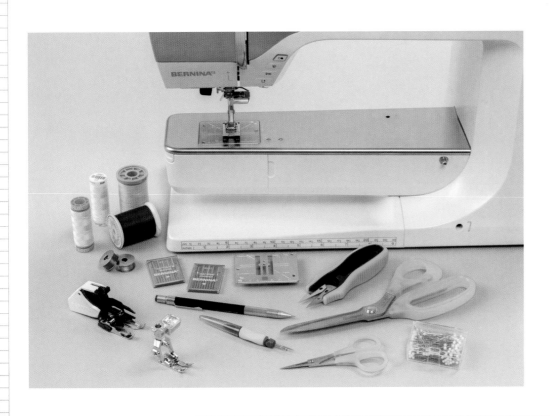

years to come. Some machines require frequent oiling while others can only be oiled by service technicians, so be sure to check your owner's manual for the proper schedule and procedures.

One important item that's often neglected is the machine needle. For machine piecing of quilts, most manufacturers recommend a size 80 Universal needle, although some machines do better with a microtex (Sharp) needle. Again, check with your manual or dealer about what's recommended for your particular machine.

If you hear your needle making a dull popping noise with each stitch, it's long past the time to throw out that needle! Replace your needle after about eight hours of sewing. That may seem like a short time, but a dull needle can damage the mechanisms under the throat plate. Why take chances with your machine for the cost of a needle?

Always attach and sew with the slide-on work table that came with your machine. It's important to have a flat surface to support your pieces as you sew. If your machine doesn't have a work table, you can purchase one from a number of companies that will customize one to fit your particular machine.

Basic Sewing Supplies

You'll want to have some basic sewing and machine supplies on hand. A few are optional, but if you have them, they can be helpful in certain situations.

- Fine silk pins, not the big quilter's pins used for basting quilt layers, for pinning patchwork pieces for sewing

- Seam ripper, used for more than ripping seams

- Thread snips, to trim loose threads

- Fabric shears

- Thread (see page 12)

- Extra bobbins for your machine

- Standard presser foot

- Quilter's ¼" presser foot (optional)

- Walking or even-feed foot (optional)

- Single-hole straight-stitch throat plate (optional)

Basic Piecing

Machine piecing is the process of sewing two pieces of fabric right sides together with a good-quality, properly tensioned, straight running stitch. The raw cut edges of the two pieces must be properly and precisely aligned before stitching.

Simple machine stitching runs from raw edge to raw edge without backstitching, because every seam sewn will eventually be crossed and secured by another seam all the way out to the binding. There are a few special instances when you'll want to backstitch, and those will be discussed as needed.

Use the standard stitch length suggested for your machine. Depending on the machine, this number can be anywhere from 1.75 to 2.5 (approximately 10 to 12 stitches per inch). Your stitches should be short enough to snugly hold your seams together at the intersections without puckering but not so small that it's difficult to rip them out.

Pins are rarely used to hold patchwork pieces together except in the case of intricate piecing. Because we're using high-quality cotton, the pieces don't slip away from each other and can be left unpinned.

The Perfect ¼" Seam Allowance

When you're following a quilt pattern, it will list the size to cut each piece. Those sizes have a ¼" seam allowance built in for all sides of each piece. But, in order for your patchwork to turn out accurately sized, you need to sew a precise ¼" seam allowance. While the idea of mastering a perfect ¼" seam allowance may seem daunting, it's the secret to frustration-free quiltmaking.

Most people assume the edge of the presser foot is the ¼" sewing guide. However, that's not necessarily true. Many people also assume that a quilter's ¼" presser foot is accurate. Unfortunately, sometimes that's not the case either. It's best to check the accuracy of the ¼" guide on your machine—and your ability to use it properly!—rather than assume it's accurate.

Teachers learn a lot from the act of teaching. I've been helping students perfect their ¼" seam guides for nearly three decades. When a student is having trouble sewing a perfect seam, the most common causes are either not having the correct width guide, not using it properly, or not aligning the fabric edges properly.

Sometimes, though, a student is doing everything well but the pieces just don't measure right when sewn. Over the years I've discovered a quirky problem to look for when all else fails. On some machines, the needle mechanism is no longer in true center. When this happens, it doesn't matter if you're aligning your edges pefectly, sewing perfectly, and using a quilter's ¼" foot or the machine's seam guide perfectly. Those machine-based guides are dependent on the needle being *in true center*. If the needle is off slightly, those guides are useless.

When this is the case, I recommend shifting needle positions or else using an applied sewing guide like the Clearly Perfect Angles guide from New Leaf Stitches. An applied sewing guide is positioned based on where the needle *actually is*, not where it should be. That key concept can make all the difference in the world for a frustrated quilter who knows she is doing what she should be to no avail. If this sounds like your situation, check your needle center position to see if it's in true center.

Take this simple test to assess the accuracy of your machine's ¼" guide and your ability to use it well.

1. Cut three 1½" x 3" strips of fabric. Make sure they are precise in width.

2. Align the raw edges perfectly.

3. Sew the strips together side by side as shown below using your ¼" sewing guide.

4. Press the two seam allowances away from the center strip.

The center strip should now measure exactly 1" from seam to seam. To see the results of your test, lay a 1"-wide ruler in the trough between the first and last strips. Don't measure the strip from the back or by laying the ruler across the width on the front to see if it is 1" wide; you won't necessarily get true results. The ruler should fit in the trough snugly the whole length of the strip. You shouldn't have to wrestle it into the space, nor should it be able to wiggle from side to side in the trough.

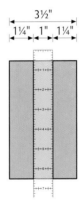

If the strip isn't precisely 1" wide, make some adjustments and retest until you can produce a consistently perfect strip test. If the center strip is too narrow, your sewn seam was too wide. If the center strip is too wide, then you've sewn too narrow a seam. Here are two solutions to help create that oh-so-important perfect ¼" seam guide.

Adjust the needle position. If your machine is capable, adjust the needle position to the right (to make a narrower seam allowance) or left (to make a wider seam allowance) a small amount at a time until you can produce a perfect strip test using your standard presser foot. **Caution:** Make sure you don't have the straight/single-stitch throat plate or the ¼" presser foot in place when sewing with the needle position out of center.

Make a masking-tape sewing guide. If you can't adjust the needle position, make a custom seam guide.

1. Lift the presser foot and raise the unthreaded needle.

2. Place a 2" x 6" piece of graph paper under the presser foot.

3. Lower the needle into the first ¼" grid line from the right edge. Adjust the paper so the grid line runs in a straight line from the needle.

4. Lower the presser foot onto the graph paper to hold it in place. Cut a piece of painter's masking tape and place it along the right edge of the graph paper, in front of the throat plate and out of the way of the feed dogs. You'll want your guide to feed your fabric into the presser foot in the correct position.

> ### ! Problem Solving
>
> Try using the Clearly Perfect Angles stitching guide from New Leaf Stitches instead of making a masking-tape guide. The package includes clear, easy-to-follow instructions for setting up the guide on your sewing machine. Clearly Perfect Angles provides an excellent guideline for sewing perfect ¼"-wide seam allowances.
>
>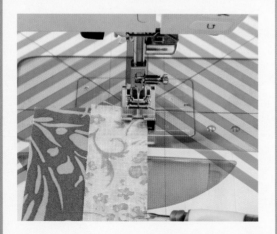

5. Sew a new test strip. If necessary, repeat and adjust the tape guide until you're able to make a perfect ¼" seam allowance. Once you have the tape guide in the correct position, build it up with several layers of tape to create a nice ridge to run your fabric edges along as you sew. You'll need to test and replace this guide periodically as it will wear out with lots of use.

> ### ! Problem Solving
>
> If you use a quilter's ¼" presser foot to sew bias edges together, like when you're sewing the long edge of two triangles together to make a half-square triangle, and notice that the bias edges pull away from each other when you're sewing, you may need to use a different presser foot. I've observed this happening in many classes I've taught. It seems that when the feed dogs are not completely covered by a narrow-width presser foot, the bias edges are not well stabilized and become hard to control. By switching to a full-sized presser foot that completely covers the feed dogs, the problem is often alleviated. If this is the case with your machine, switch to another method for sewing a ¼" seam allowance.
>
>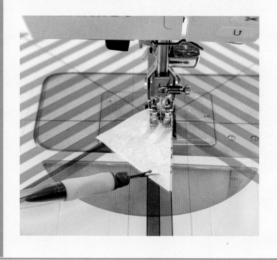

Stitching Tips and Tricks

The following tips and tricks may be classified as those little things that can make a surprising world of difference. Some of them may leave you scratching your head and wondering why it matters, but you'll be surprised how they can help when you try them. That's quite frequently the reaction I get from my students, "Wow—who'd have thunk?" Give them a try!

Leaders and Enders

This is a great trick that has become quite popular over the years. Begin by sewing across a folded strip of fabric (the "leader") about 1" to 1½" wide. Stop with your presser foot and needle down in the front edge of the leader. Do not remove the leader! Sew your first set of pieces together, and keep right on chain sewing (see "Chain Sewing" on page 50) all of your pieces. End your stitching session by sewing across a second fabric scrap (the "ender") and stopping with the presser foot and needle down in front of the ender. Again, do not remove the ender. Cut your sewn pieces from the back of the ender.

Leader

A good source of ready-made leaders and enders is leftover prepared binding cut into short segments. I always have multiple projects going at once, so I feed parts of other projects through in place of leader and ender strips. There are several benefits to this little trick.

- After you have leaders in place, you'll no longer have to start with loose thread tails that must be held tight.

- When you end by sewing across a second scrap with your needle down in the front edge, you'll be ready to start your next session of sewing.

- Your fabric will no longer be eaten or mangled at the beginning of the seam.

- Leaders and enders eliminate bird's nests of threads on the bottom of your good seam. Any such problems are on the fabric scraps instead of your pieced units.

- If the first few stitches your machine makes are a bit rough, they'll be on the leader, not on the piece going into your quilt.

- Many machines sew a better stitch once the presser foot and feed dogs are engaged with fabric.

- You'll reduce thread waste dramatically!

- You don't need to clip thread tails from every seam you sew.

Blue-Ribbon Skills

Use the fabric leader to protect the points of triangles you want to sew. By placing the triangle tips on the leader, you keep them safe from being mangled or pulled under the throat plate. Be careful that the points aren't so far onto the leader that the triangle is sewn to it. Once sewing is under way, place the points of subsequent triangle pairs on top of the points of the previously sewn pair. Be sure to lift the presser foot slightly to position the points correctly.

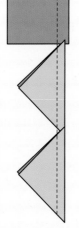

Chain Sewing

Chain sewing is an assembly-line approach to stitching. The idea is to save time by sewing as many seams as possible, one right after the other, rather than stopping and starting after each seam is sewn. In conjunction with leaders and enders discussed in the previous section, chain sewing is very time efficient.

Begin with a leader, followed by your first unit. Stop with your needle down in the front edge of the seam you just sewed. Don't pull the unit from the sewing area and don't raise the needle. Lift the presser foot slightly and place the next unit into position, leaving a small space between it and the previously sewn unit. Lower the presser foot and stitch.

Continue sewing in the same fashion with all the pieces, creating a "kite tail" of sewn units connected by small twists of thread. Finish by sewing across an ender, stopping with the needle and presser foot down in the front edge.

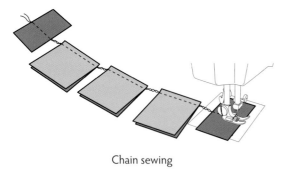

Chain sewing

Once you've sewn everything needed for this step, cut the kite tail from the back of the ender, cut apart the pieces, and continue with the next step in the construction process.

> ### ! Problem Solving
>
> Some machines refuse to handle points well. Try switching to a single-hole/straight-stitch throat plate. The small round opening helps prevent points from being pulled under. Please note that your needle *must* be in the center position when using this throat plate.

The Better Finger

This is a nifty little trick that can reap rewards. Use the point of a seam ripper, bamboo skewer, sewing stiletto, or any other slender, pointy tool to gently secure and guide your fabric pieces just up to the needle. This is especially helpful with smaller or more intricate piecing. Our fingers are generally too large to get close enough to the needle safely while holding everything in place. I actually prefer this trick to pinning pieces together. I find that removing pins just before sewing over them can actually shift the fabric layers slightly sideways and out of alignment. The better finger is simply lifted out of the way so no shifting occurs.

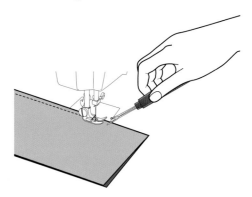

Use seam ripper to guide fabric while stitching.

The other benefit to using a better finger in this fashion is that it lets you exert less downward pressure on the fabric pieces, especially strips, as you gently feed them under the needle. I see too many quilters inadvertently keeping a tight hold on their strip sets as they sew them, thus exerting a gentle backward tug as the feed dogs are also pulling the strips toward the needle. The result is that the crosswise grain of the strips can stretch a bit and result in a slightly curved strip set. The lighter guidance of the seam ripper provides a less heavy-handed approach.

The better finger also acts as an aid in holding matching intersections in place without the need for pins. Nest the seams and use the tool to hold the nesting secure up to the presser foot. You can also use it to lift layers to realign edges as necessary as you approach the needle.

You'll find that with practice, eventually you won't feel comfortable or in control sewing without a seam ripper or other tool in your hand.

Easing

Sometimes you'll find that two pieces to be sewn together aren't quite the same length. Generally, if it's a big difference, you need to go back and correct whatever is wrong. Is one or more of the seams that's already sewn to the unit too large or too small? If so, fix the problem.

If the discrepancy is small, you can "ease" in the fullness of the larger piece without puckers by putting it on the bottom when sewing. Use pins to help disperse the fullness if necessary. The feed dogs will ease in that bit of fullness easily. If sewn with the larger piece on top, the presser foot can push the fullness into a pleat.

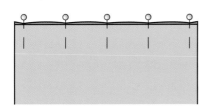

Ease fullness evenly
along the seam, using pins.

Matching Intersections

We all want our seams to match, our points to be impressively sharp, and everything to fit nicely without feeling the need for hair pulling or heavy drinking. Here are some tried-and-true techniques to make all your intersections brag worthy.

Nesting Seams

We've already discussed the idea of nesting seams in "Pressing" (page 33). It's the primary way to match seam intersections without using pins. By pressing seam allowances that will meet at an intersection in opposite directions, you can better guarantee nice sharp points and corners. Conversely, if all seam allowances were pressed in the same direction, you'd have at least six stacked layers of fabric to sew and bump across. It's rare for points to remain matched in such a situation. They tend to slip off the pile of bulk to one side or the other.

When you nest seams, the ridges of the opposing seam allowances are forced tight next to each other. This is what creates those perfect points you want.

Opposing seams

It's important to nest diagonal seams as well as straight seams. When diagonal seams meet, they generally form points or peaks. If they're not matched well, they stand out like a sore thumb in a completed quilt block. Always stitch from the corner where the diagonals meet.

Begin stitching.

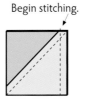

Ensuring that diagonal seams nest is a good example of why it's so important to take the extra time and effort to create a pressing plan.

Blue-Ribbon Skills

Whether nesting simple seams or intricate piecing, whenever possible, sew with the raw edges of the seam allowances on the top layer facing *toward* the needle.

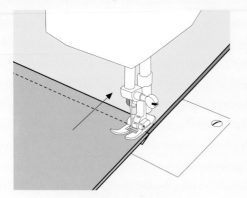

Face top seam allowances toward the needle.

You may instinctively think it's easier for the presser foot to glide over the seam allowances if the raw edges face away from the needle. While that may be true, the reality is that a presser foot often pushes the top layer slightly forward toward you. When that happens the intersection is pushed slightly out of alignment, resulting in points that don't match. But, if the raw edges are facing the needle, the ridge of the bottom layer stops this forward momentum, resulting in a very nice, tight intersection.

Point-to-Point Sewing

When sewing a long seam that crosses over many intersections, first pick up and visually check the intersections of each piece to make sure they'll all fit together nicely. Make adjustments if one piece is longer than the other. If there's a small discrepancy in lengths, put the fuller piece on the bottom to ease it into place. For larger problems, find the source of trouble, and go back and correct it.

Once all is well, match and nest the first intersection only. Sew up to this point and stop with your needle down a thread or two past the intersection. Now, adjust and nest the next intersection. Sew just past

it and stop. Continue on in this fashion. It's much less stressful to worry about one intersection at a time instead of trying to match all of them at once.

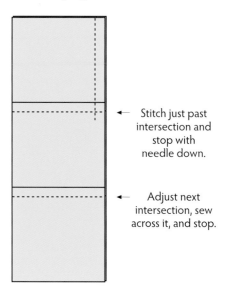

← Stitch just past intersection and stop with needle down.

← Adjust next intersection, sew across it, and stop.

Sewing from the Square

When sewing a triangle onto a square, it's best to align the right-angle corners of the two pieces first. Then position the pieces so you can sew them on your machine, starting from the matched right-angle corner. The feed dogs handle the triangle point better when it follows the seam rather than when it starts the seam. Ending with the point keeps it from being mangled.

Start stitching at right-angle corner.

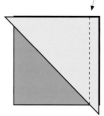

The X Intersection

Unless you sew only squares and rectangles, you'll eventually come across an X intersection. This occurs when you sew across a triangle point that falls on the edge of another seam. The point where the seams meet forms an X and should measure ¼" from the edge. If it doesn't, take a look at what went wrong and fix it. Sometimes you can trim the excess to ¼" from the edge, but check it before you start trimming.

The goal is to sew precisely from the edge so the stitching falls a thread's distance to the right of the X. If you sew directly through the center of the X, you'll find when you turn the pieces to the right side that the points are slightly buried in the fold of the seam allowance. By sewing a thread's distance to the right of center, you allow the point to be fully exposed. If you sew too far right toward the raw edge, you risk floating your point. If you sew to the left of the X, you lop off the point. Neither scenario is desirable.

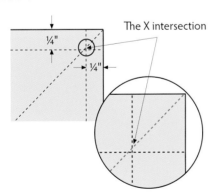

The X intersection

¼" ¼" ¼"

Positioning Pins

There are times, such as when many points meet at one spot or the seams that meet are coming from opposite angles, when you must pin an intersection. In these cases, rather than pinning directly through the intersection, use positioning pins to secure the intersection.

To do this, match all seams and points manually and then secure pins slightly to the left and right of the intersection to hold the layers in place. Because removing pins can shift layers, it's important to keep pins out of the intersection itself. By placing pins on either side of it, you can secure the intersection so it doesn't shift when you pull the pins out.

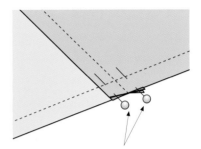

Secure pins to either side
of intersection.

Use your better finger (page 50) to help guide the pieces as you slowly sew to just short of the intersection. Stop with the needle down and remove the first pin. Stitch across the intersection. Stop with the needle down and remove the second pin. Continue stitching.

Partial Basting

Instead of pins, use either hand or machine basting to secure an intersection before sewing the final seam. Place the basting inside the ¼" seam allowance so it won't interfere with the actual seam.

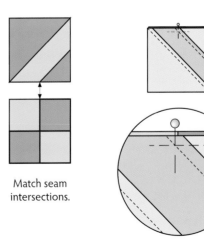

Match seam
intersections.

Spear intersection with pin.

"Candy Dots," pieced and appliquéd by Donna Lynn Thomas and quilted by Denise Mariano,
 from *Patchwork Palette*

Special Sewing Techniques

Beyond sewing together simple squares and triangles, there are many other sewing techniques you'll encounter as you want to try different patterns. Following, you'll find some of the most common techniques used in quiltmaking.

Straight-Grain Strip Piecing

This simple technique eliminates the need to cut and sew many individual squares or rectangles, thereby speeding up the assembly process. For example, let's take a look at a simple Nine Patch block. Without strip piecing, you'd need to cut nine individual squares and sew them together one by one to make each block. If we break the block into three horizontal rows, we can see that rows 1 and 3 are the same but different from row 2.

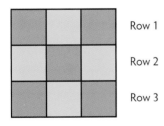

Row 1

Row 2

Row 3

Nine-patch block

Instead of squares, cut strips of fabric the same width as you'd cut the squares. See "Cutting Strips" (page 21). Sew the strips together side by side to make strip sets as shown above right. Press each seam one at a time as you go—don't try to press them all at once after the strip set is assembled or you'll have an ironing nightmare trying to manage all those flippy-floppy strips. It's much easier to tame each seam with the iron one at a time, add the next

strip, press, and continue. As a result, each seam will be straight and true. You'll need one strip set configured for rows 1 and 3 and a second strip set configured for row 2.

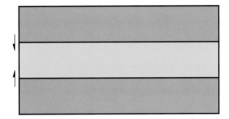

Rows 1 and 3 strip set

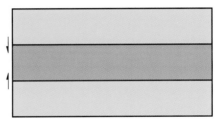

Row 2 strip set

Blue-Ribbon Skills

When sewing strip sets, use a light-handed approach feeding the strips under the presser foot so the crosswise grain isn't stretched. When pressing strip sets, press perpendicularly to the seam, nudging the strip over the seam allowance. This also prevents stretching of the crosswise grain, which runs parallel to the seam in most cases.

⚠ Problem Solving

If you find your strip sets end up as curved rainbows instead of straight arrows, consider the following:

- Try using a seam ripper or pointed awl to guide your strips as you sew. Sometimes overhandling the strips or the weight of your hands on the strips can stretch and bend the cross grain on the edges.

- Try sewing every other strip in a strip set from the opposite end to help prevent curvature.

- Sometimes working with half-length (21") strips makes it easier to control and handle them gently, resulting in less curvature.

- Check the thread tension on your machine. If it's too tight, it can pull up the seam, resulting in those unwanted "rainbow" strip sets.

Crosscut the sewn strip sets into segments equal to the cut size of the squares. To cut segments:

1. Make a clean-cut edge along the short end of the strip set. Make this cut at a right angle to the seams by aligning a horizontal ruler line on the seams at the same time that you trim the end.

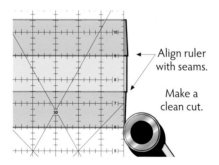

Align ruler with seams.

Make a clean cut.

2. Turn the strip set and position the ruler marking on the clean edge at the required cutting distance. Align an interior horizontal ruler line on the seams to ensure a right-angle cut every time.

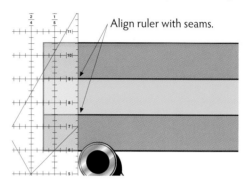

Align ruler with seams.

3. After several cuts, when you can no longer align the measuring lines and the seam line at the same time, you may need to re-trim the edge of the strip set.

The cut segments are the block rows. Now it's a simple matter to sew the two types of segments together to complete a block.

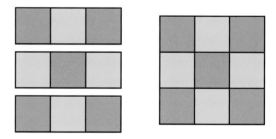

Use strip sets whenever possible for piecing blocks and quilts. You'll find some strip sets to be very simple and others quite complex, involving varied strip and segment widths. Despite this, the process and concept remains the same as with the simple nine patch example.

On-Point Strip Sets

If you're making strip sets for on-point patchwork units, refer to "Cutting Diagonal Measurements with the On-Point Ruler" (page 30) to use the On-Point Ruler to cut the strips so the final units will measure evenly on the diagonals. First, decide the finished diagonal measurement of each square in the unit. Then cut strips at that mark using the On-Point Ruler and sew your strip set together. Cut segments at the desired diagonal width and sew your unit together.

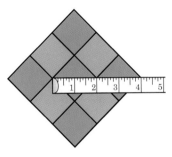

Determine finished
square measurement.

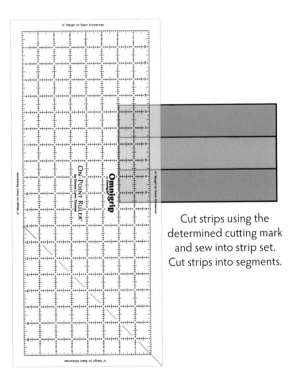

Cut strips using the
determined cutting mark
and sew into strip set.
Cut strips into segments.

The process for cutting and sewing the strip sets and crosscutting the segments is the same as with a regular rotary-cutting ruler. Only the measurement is different.

Half-Square-Triangle Units

Half-square-triangle units are pieced squares composed of two half-square triangles. Although there are many, many innovative ways and tools to make these units, here are two simple methods that require a minimum of equipment and effort.

Method 1

Cut two different-colored squares in half diagonally to make two pairs of half-square triangles. Sew opposite-colored triangles together along their long bias edges. Press the seam allowances to one side.

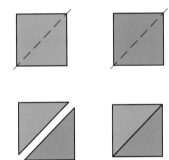

Method 2

This method avoids sewing two raw bias edges together as in method 1. Rather than cutting the squares into triangles, draw a diagonal line precisely from corner to corner on the wrong side of the lightest square, using a fine-line mechanical pencil. Draw two more lines, each ¼" from the center line. Place the squares right sides together. Sew on the ¼" lines, and then cut on the center diagonal line to make two half-square-triangle units. Press.

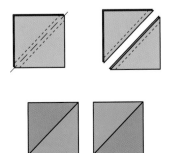

Oversized Units

Many times, the half-square-triangle units aren't terribly accurate because stretching occurs in the sewing and pressing steps—regardless of the method used. Many people prefer to make slightly oversized units and trim them to a perfect cut size after the sewing and pressing steps are complete. The result is perfectly sized half-square-triangle units every time with a minimum of effort. I like to use the Bias Square® ruler for trimming the half-square-triangle units to size, but any square ruler with a 45°-angle line will do the trick.

To make oversized units, add 1" to the desired *finished* size and cut squares this measurement. Then proceed with either method 1 or 2 to make your half-square-triangle units. Trim them to the finished size + ½".

1. Place the diagonal line of the ruler on the seam of the half-square-triangle unit with the trim size measurement inside the lower edge of the unit.

2. Trim the top two edges.

3. Turn the unit around and place the trim measurement of the ruler on the freshly cut edges and the diagonal line back on the seam. Trim the second set of edges.

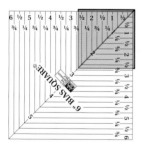

Place diagonal line of ruler on seam line. Trim first two sides.

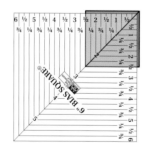

Align desired measurement on previously cut edge and diagonal line on seam. Trim remaining sides.

On-Point Half-Square-Triangle Units

You can use the same two methods described in "Half-Square-Triangle Units" on page 57 to make either precise or oversized half-square-triangle units that will measure evenly on the diagonal. Use the On-Point Ruler to cut the squares. For precise cuts, add ½" to the desired diagonal measurement. Cut squares this size and use method 1 or 2 to make your half-square-triangle units.

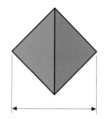

Finished diagonal of half-square-triangle unit.

For oversized units, add 1" to the desired diagonal measurement and cut squares at that mark using the On-Point Ruler. Again, use either method 1 or 2 to make oversized half-square-triangle units. In the same fashion as above, use the diagonal line on the corner of the On-Point Ruler or the On-Point Square to trim the half-square-triangle units to their desired diagonal measurement. Add nothing for trimming.

Folded Corners

This technique has multiple names, so you may know it by sew-and-flip or even another term. The basic idea of folded corners is to sew a square of fabric to the corner of a larger parent square or rectangle (see page 23) along the diagonal, and then fold over the smaller square to duplicate a corner triangle. Use the following simple process to make folded-corner units.

1. Determine the finished size of the corner triangle where it falls on the side of the main unit. Add ½" to this measurement and cut a square this size. In the example given, you'd cut a 2½" square to sew onto the 4" finished parent square.

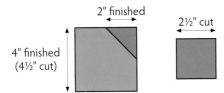

2. Draw a diagonal line on the wrong side of the smaller corner square. This line must be very fine and accurate, running exactly from corner to corner. To keep the fabric from shifting as you mark, place the square on a sandpaper board or super-fine sandpaper. To further reduce shifting, hold your pencil at a 45° angle so the point doesn't drag in the weave of the fabric. Carefully place the smaller square on the corner of the larger parent unit with right sides together. Sew just *to the right* of the marked line so that your stitching sits next to the line with no visible space between. Always sew with the corner that will be trimmed away positioned to the right of your needle.

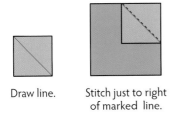

Draw line.   Stitch just to right of marked line.

3. Press the small square back over the corner, right side facing up, and check it for accuracy. Be careful not to stretch it. It should lie exactly on the corner of the parent unit. If it doesn't, check the accuracy of the marked line or your sewing and adjust as needed. If the square comes up short of the corner, you may need to sew a thread's width closer to the corner of the unit. If the square is too big for the corner, check to make sure you're sewing exactly from corner to corner and your pieces are lined up properly. If there's consistent trouble, check the accuracy of the corner-square

Blue-Ribbon Skills

Consider using the Clearly Perfect Angles stitching template from New Leaf Stitches instead of drawing diagonal lines on each square. It's designed specifically with this purpose in mind. The package includes clear, easy-to-follow instructions for setting up the guide on your sewing machine. Online video tutorials are also available on the company's website: NewLeafStitches.com.

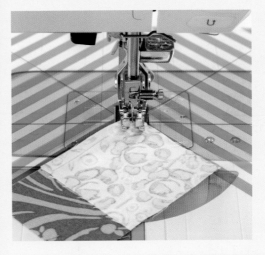

size, the parent-unit size, the drawn line, or your sewing to find and correct the source of the problem. Each seam must be accurate in order for your final unit to finish at the size it's meant to be.

Fold square over corner.

4. Trim away both extra layers of fabric under the top corner triangle, trimming ¼" from the stitching line.

Here are some additional tips to help ensure your success with the folded-corners technique.

- Use an open-toe or clear presser foot so you can see to place the first corner precisely in front of the needle.

- Use a straight-stitch throat plate, if you have one, to keep corners from being sucked into the larger hole of a regular throat plate and mangled.

- Lift your presser foot slightly to place each piece under the foot. Running it under the lowered presser foot without lifting can misalign the top piece.

- Pin through the layers in the right corner to keep them from shifting as you sew if you experience a problem. (Some machines lose control of the bias edges as they sew and pivot the pieces out of alignment.) Because the pin is positioned out of the way of the oncoming needle, you don't need to remove it to prevent needle breakage.

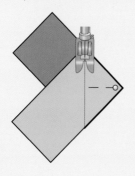

Partial Seams

In some quilt blocks, there's no clear-cut type of block assembly, such as four-patch assembly or sewing rows. Usually this happens when the final seams don't run completely from one side of the block to another. In this instance, you'll need to sew a partial seam to get things started, then go back and finish the partial seam at the end of your block assembly.

Take a look at this Hex block. The pieced units are built onto the center square in a circular fashion, ending where they began.

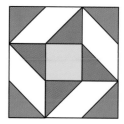

Hex block

Sew the first unit to the center square with a half (partial) seam. Once in place, the rest of the units can be added completely one at a time as shown. When the fourth unit is sewn in place, go back and finish the rest of the seam on the first unit.

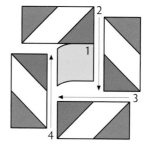 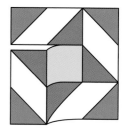

Six- and Eight-Pointed Stars and Centers

While most machine piecing is sewn from raw edge to raw edge, stars and multiple-pointed centers are the exception. These seams are sewn from point to point, ¼" in from each edge. Let's use a LeMoyne Star as an example.

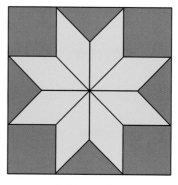

LeMoyne Star

1. On the wrong side of each diamond, mark ¼" crosshairs at each corner using a fine-line mechanical pencil.

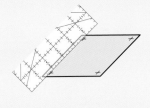
2. Arrange the diamonds as they'll be sewn together.

3. Pin the diamonds into pairs, matching the ¼" crosshairs.

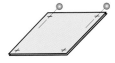

Pin diamonds into pairs.

4. Sew each pair together from the center point out to the edge of the block, using the securing stitch on your machine at the center point. If your machine doesn't have this function, start your stitching in the seam allowance near the point and sew to the first point. Stop with your needle down precisely in the ¼" intersection. Pivot your piece and stitch to the outside point, and then use

the securing stitch or backstitch a few stitches to secure the point.

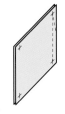

Start here. →

Sew to mark at center. Stop with needle down.

Pivot and sew to next ¼" point, backstitch, and remove.

5. Press the seam allowances of each pair so they'll consistently flow in either a clockwise or counter-clockwise direction.

6. In the same fashion, sew the pairs of diamonds together to make half blocks.

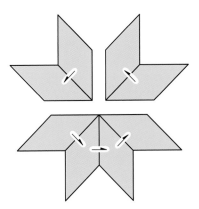

Check the center seam of each half block before sewing them together. On the right side, the points should all meet sharply ¼" from the raw edge. Make any adjustments at this point.

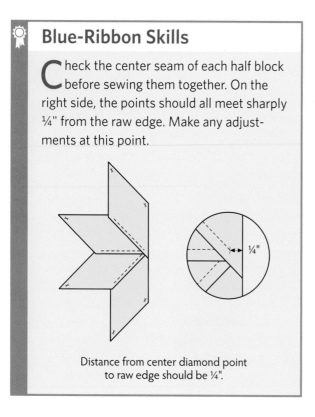

Distance from center diamond point to raw edge should be ¼".

7. Pin the two star halves together, using nesting seams and positioning pins to help secure the center. Stitch from the ¼" point on one side of the star to the other side.

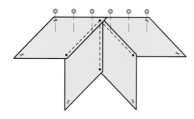

Secure center point with positioning pins.

8. Even though the final seam completely crosses the center, you should still be able to release a few stitches in the center so all the seam allowances continue in the circular direction.

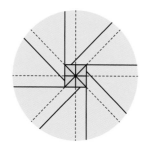

Set-In Seams

Set-in seams are necessary when the only way to add a piece to a block is by stitching it in place in two steps. Sticking with the LeMoyne Star example, follow these steps to successfully set in the squares and triangles needed to finish the block.

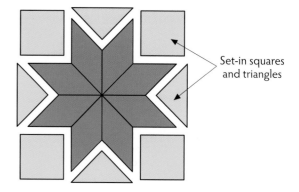

Set-in squares and triangles

1. On the wrong side of the squares and triangles, make ¼" crosshairs as you did previously with the diamonds (page 61).

2. Arrange the pieces as they'll be sewn.

3. Begin by pinning only one side of the two-step seam. Use the pins to match the ¼" crosshairs on the two pieces to be sewn. Fold any pressed seam allowances out of the way so as to not include them in the new seam.

4. Backstitch into the first corner, pivot, and stitch out to the outside ¼" crosshair.

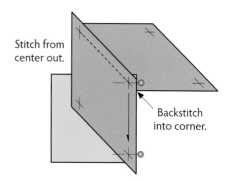

Stitch from center out.

Backstitch into corner.

5. Rotate your piece so the second leg of the seam is aligned with its mate. Sew from the inside corner to the outer edge in the same fashion as the first seam.

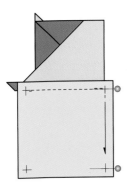

Twist second half of seam into
position; pin at corners and
stitch from center out.

6. Continue sewing all the set-in seams around the block.

Curved Piecing

Curved seams are composed of two types of curves: convex and concave. It's easy to remember the difference; concave curves "cave in" while the convex curves bulge out.

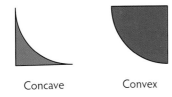

Concave   Convex

1. The concave piece must be stretched to fit around the bulgy convex piece. To allow this, clip into the seam allowance of the concave piece. Make your clips perpendicular to the edge of the fabric and about every ½" to start. Make fewer clips on a wide gentle curve. You can always add more clips later if necessary. Don't clip any further in from the edge than about ³⁄₁₆". It's not necessary to clip the convex piece.

Make ³⁄₁₆"-deep clips
along concave curves.

2. Mark the center of the convex piece by folding it in half *wrong sides together* and finger-pressing a crease in the center of the curved seam. Finger-press a crease in the center of the concave piece by pressing it in half *right sides together*.

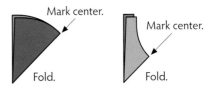

Mark center.   Mark center.

Fold.   Fold.

Or, if your template has centering marks, transfer those to your fabric pieces.

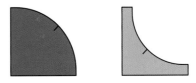

Use template to mark center of fabric piece.

3. Arrange the pieces right sides together so the creases of the two pieces cup together neatly. Pin the creases.

4. Pin the two corners and adjust with more clips if necessary in order for the units to fit well. Some people are happy with just three pins. Others use more pins along the length of the seam, dispersing the fullness evenly. Try it both ways on practice pieces to learn what you prefer.

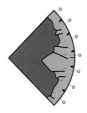

Pin concave piece
to convex piece with
center guidelines matching. Turn
over and sew with the concave
piece on the bottom.

5. Sew slowly and carefully, using your seam-ripper point to align the edges as you go. If you sew with the concave piece on the bottom, the unit will tend to cup up around the sewing needle, allowing you to more easily guide and feed it under the needle.

About the Author

Photography by Katie Lynn Thomas

Donna has been sewing since the age of four and quilting since 1975. She began teaching in 1981, and since 1988 has been a National Quilting Association certified teacher for basic quilt-making (NQACT). While an Army wife, she lived in Germany for four years and taught routinely at a German quilt shop and various guilds throughout the country. Long out of the Army, the Thomases have settled in Kansas for good. Donna still teaches nationally.

The author of many previous titles with Martingale, Donna's books include *Scrappy Duos*, *Flip Your Way to Fabulous Quilts*, *Patchwork Palette*, and *On-Point Patchwork*. She has also contributed articles on various quilt-related subjects to numerous publications over the years. She is the designer of the Omnigrid On-Point Ruler and the On-Point Square.

Her greatest joys are her husband, Terry, and their two sons, Joe and Pete. Equally dear to her heart is Joe's wife, Katie, and their most-perfect-in-every-way daughters, Charlotte and Alexandra.

Donna and Terry provide staff assistance to their three cats, Max, Jack, and Skittles, and a kiddie pool and ear scratches to one sunny golden retriever, Ellie. All the quilts in their house are lovingly "pre-furred."